Thornton Wilder's
The Skin of Our Teeth

T0268885

"Ladies and gentlemen, I'm not going to play this particular scene tonight."

– Sabina

Thornton Wilder's *The Skin of Our Teeth* (1942) telescopes an audacious stretch of western history and mythology into a family drama, showing how the course of human events operates like theatre itself: constantly mutable, vanishing and beginning again.

Kyle Gillette explores Wilder's extraordinary play in three parts. Part I unpacks the play's singular yet deeply interconnected place in theatre history, comparing its metatheatrics to those of Stein, Pirandello and Brecht, and finding its anticipation of American fantasias in the works of Vogel and Kushner. Part II turns to the play's many historic and mythic sources, and examines its concentration of western progress and power into the model of a white, American upper-middle-class nuclear family. Part III takes a longer view, tangling with the play's philosophical stakes.

Gillette magnifies the play's ideas and connections, teasing out historical, theoretical and philosophical questions on behalf of readers, scholars and audience members alike.

Kyle Gillette is Associate Professor and Director of Theatre at Trinity University, San Antonio.

The Fourth Wall

The Fourth Wall series is a growing collection of short books on famous plays. Its compact format perfectly suits the kind of fresh, engaging criticism that brings a play to life.

Each book in this series selects one play or musical as its subject and approaches it from an original angle, seeking to shed light on an old favourite or break new ground on a modern classic. These lively, digestible books are a must for anyone looking for new ideas on the major works of modern theatre.

Also available in this series:

Coming soon:

Thornton Wilder's
The Skin of Our Teeth

Kyle Gillette

Routledge
Taylor & Francis Group

LONDON AND NEW YORK

First published 2016
by Routledge
2 Park Square, Milton Park, Abingdon, Oxon OX14 4RN

and by Routledge
711 Third Avenue, New York, NY 10017

Routledge is an imprint of the Taylor & Francis Group, an informa business

© 2016 Kyle Gillette

British Library Cataloguing-in-Publication Data
A catalogue record for this book is available from
the British Library

Library of Congress Cataloguing-in-Publication Data
A catalog record for this title has been requested

ISBN: 9781138185623 (pbk)
ISBN: 9781315644349 (ebk)

Typeset in Bembo
by Out of House Publishing

Contents

PART III
Metaphysics 63

Note on the text

All quotations from the play are taken from Thornton Wilder, *The Skin of Our Teeth* (New York: Perennial Classics, 2003).

Introduction

Thornton Wilder wrote his apocalyptic play *The Skin of Our Teeth* in 1942, just as the United States entered the Second World War. The play's structure is riddled with interruptions that jar spectators between multiple frames of reality. Written in the midst of theatrical modernism's most vibrant experiments with form, *The Skin of Our Teeth*'s success on Broadway was both bizarre and fitting: Wilder distilled modernist metatheatrical elements common to Gertrude Stein, Luigi Pirandello and Bertolt Brecht into an approachable fantasia on western civilization. His playful exploration of metatheatre and history anticipates some of the most interesting works of the past half-century, such as Caryl Churchill's *Cloud Nine* (1978), Tony Kushner's *Angels in America* (1993) and Suzan-Lori Parks's *The America Play* (1994): plays that connect macrocosmic stakes to personal longing and that exploit the very stuff of theatre to investigate the deep structures of civilization, time and history.

At the heart of *The Skin of Our Teeth*'s power and influence is its audacious collage of history and myth. Exuberantly anachronistic, the play stages the end of the world three times: by ice, flood and war. Act I begins with the invention of the wheel and alphabet, and ends with the advancing glaciers and dying of the fire. Act II starts with wealth and decadence at the Atlantic City Boardwalk and ends in a biblical flood. Act III begins in the aftermath of a devastating seven-year war and ends in philosophical reflection and rebirth. Yet everything that befalls humankind focuses on the Antrobus family (*anthropos* = 'human' in Greek; *omnibus* = 'all' in Latin). The Antrobuses are simultaneously mythic and a 'typical' American nuclear family: George (Adam) and Maggie (Eve), their son Henry (Cain) and daughter Gladys, their maid, their pet mammoth and dinosaur.

Throughout, the play falls apart as actors break character, stage managers interrupt the action and set pieces fly away. The play's scope is too much for its structure to contain. Colliding burlesque and melodrama, realism and extravaganza, comedy and philosophy, the play perpetually works itself out in front of us. Wilder explores the vastness and repetitions of history through the energy of a theatrical production whose illusions are never stable. He also points skyward, beyond what the play can hope to reproduce: the cosmos, the celestial bodies, the thoughts of philosophers that infuse us and transcend generations. By showing the theatrical apparatus try, and fail, to swallow such impossible vastness, Wilder asks fundamental questions about representation, history and being.

This book explores the play through three interconnected lenses: as metatheatre, as metahistory and as metaphysics. By 'metatheatre', I mean most directly the trope of staging theatre within theatre – as in the so-called 'Mousetrap' scene of Shakespeare's *Hamlet*, wherein the elements of theatrical representation both help us 'catch the conscience of the king' and gesture toward the complex operations of witnessing, narration and visual representation so fundamental to theatre. I also use 'metatheatre' here to refer to the exposed apparatus of theatre – theatre that deliberately makes its theatricality (including its limitations) apparent and part of the work. The two chapters of Part I ('Metatheatre and failure', 'Metatheatre and modernism') analyse *The Skin of Our Teeth*'s use of metatheatre and its important role in the twentieth century's development of formal experimentation in mainstream theatre. I suggest that Wilder distilled theatrical modernism's most significant metatheatrical energies into what became a kind of *ur*-play, or model script, for metatheatrical fantasias of the late twentieth century. Wilder's interruptions make the familiar strange, like the epic theatre of Bertolt Brecht, yet paradoxically invite a bittersweet empathy – not for individual characters but for the deaths and rebirths of human cultures. Wilder draws together the forces of modernist metatheatre to create a new kind of apocalyptic American play whose stakes are simultaneously historical and metaphysical, political and personal. The play shows us how much the world outside is like theatre and how we can more deeply recognize the theatrical nature of its cataclysms and renewals.

By invoking the word 'metahistory' I follow Hayden White's use of the term to mean a kind of historiography that looks at the 'deep structure' of history itself: the ways we imagine history; the ideologies undergirding the historian's (or playwright's) narratives about progress; the creation myths that justify power (White, 1973). Part II (comprising 'Metahistory and myth', and 'Metahistory and myopia') unpacks *The Skin of Our Teeth*'s historic and mythic narratives (and metanarratives), ranging from biblical and Greek characters to Napoleonic costumes and postwar Americana. Different strains of ancient and modern history and myth interweave through the play, challenging and incorporating each other, ultimately complicating any unified, linear, teleological notion of historical progress. Wilder also invents minds shaped by their places in history, myopic in their tendency to make from the past a story about themselves. The play concentrates western progress and power into the model of a white, modern, American upper-middle-class nuclear family. Wilder's necessarily failed attempt to stage everything that has ever existed shows not only the limits of history (as told by the victors, or at least survivors) but also the power of imagination to invoke or challenge the lineages that shape us as particular individuals.

Ultimately, underlying his metatheatre and metahistory, Wilder sketches a kind of metaphysics, a philosophical orientation whose object is the nature and purpose of being. Part III ('Metaphysics on parade'; 'Metaphysics and the end of history') zooms out to engage the play's philosophical stakes. Wilder's play ends with a parade of philosophical quotes from Spinoza, Plato, Aristotle and Genesis. This procession suggests humans' temporary place in a river of thoughts that shapes us. These particular thinkers articulate visions of reality's deep structure and our moral place in the universe. They also reinforce a linear, teleological paradigm of history. In the final chapter, I trace how Wilder gives form to western linear history and eschatology – its orientation toward apocalypse and final judgment – but then upends it, showing how the course of human events, particularly through environmental catastrophes and war, operates like theatre itself: constantly mutable, vanishing and beginning again.

Part I

Metatheatre

1

Metatheatre and failure

As soon as a projected slide show begins the play with 'NEWS EVENTS OF THE WORLD', *The Skin of Our Teeth* announces its reality as split. The announcer situates the action we are about to see as part of a storytelling kind of theatre quite different from the domestic realism, lighthearted comedy or Broadway musical dominant in 1942 American theatre. Sabina the maid begins the first scene with an introduction to the characters and milieu of the Antrobus household. She dusts while telling us about the family, revealing its secrets and establishing a direct relationship with the audience (long before the actress playing her, Miss Somerset, first interrupts to tell us what she really thinks about the play).

From the start, the Antrobus house is beset by theatrical malfunctions. As Sabina begins, a *'fragment of the right wall leans precariously over the stage. SABINA looks at it nervously and it slowly rights itself.'* A few lines later it *'flies up into the lofts. SABINA is struck dumb with surprise.'* These early technical failures compound when Mrs Antrobus misses her cue. Sabina says the cue line again: 'Don't forget that a few years ago we came through the depression by The Skin of Our

Teeth. One more tight squeeze like that and where will we be?'. Finally, the stage manager Mr Fitzpatrick has no choice but to tell Miss Somerset to 'Make up something!'. But Miss Somerset is not that kind of actress. She is not comfortable with improvisation and has little regard for the play: 'I can't invent any words for this play, and I'm glad I can't. I hate this play and every word in it.' She finds it perplexing and baulks at its scope: 'As for me, I don't understand a single word of it, anyway, – all about the troubles the human race has gone through, there's a subject for you.'

Miss Somerset has a special impatience for the play's central conceit of collapsing ordinary modern people with ancient sources: 'Besides, the author hasn't made up his silly mind as to whether we're all living back in caves or in New Jersey today, and that's the way it is all the way through.' Mrs Antrobus finally enters (late) and asks Sabina if she has milked the mammoth. 'I don't understand a word of this play. Yes, I've milked the mammoth.' When Sabina later has to denigrate Judge Moses with 'The Ten Commandments – FAUGH!!!', Miss Somerset says, 'That's the worst line I've ever had to say on any stage.' But through her confusion, she also allows the audience to see the play through her eyes as she gives signposts of discovery: 'Now that you audience are listening to this, too, I understand it a little better.' Still, the sense of being trapped remains in the sheer fact of repetition inherent in theatre: 'I wish eleven o'clock were here; I don't want to be dragged through this whole play again.'

Miss Somerset has a sense of personal decorum that contrasts sharply with the actions of Sabina and the stakes of the play. She dislikes both dark realism and the play's encyclopedic pastiche; she pines for traditional plays with romantic love stories. Her generally bourgeois and philistine tastes throw the play's darker themes into sharp relief and guide us through them. When she does understand elements of Wilder's play (for the first time in its presumably long run) she objects to its representations of abjection or suffering. When Moses, Homer, the Muses, Socrates and Hippocrates seek shelter in the Antrobus home against the oncoming ice age, Miss Somerset suddenly '*drops the play*' midline and, scandalized, crosses to the proscenium. 'Oh, *I* see what this part of the play means now! This means refugees.' Leaning against the proscenium arch, she '*bursts into tears*' and says 'Oh, I don't like it. I don't like it.' She tries to assuage whatever guilty discomfort the audience may have too:

> Ladies and gentlemen! Don't take this play serious. The world's not coming to an end. You know it's not. People exaggerate! Most people really have enough to eat and a roof over their heads. Nobody actually starves – you can always eat grass or something. That ice-business – why, it was a long, long time ago. Besides they were only savages. Savages don't love their families – not like we do.

As the USA entered the Second World War, with horrific news pouring in from Europe and Asia along with evidence of genocide on an unprecedented scale, American audiences were all too unsettled by the NEWS EVENTS OF THE WORLD and had to choose to look or look away. Pearl Harbor ended war-weary isolationism with a reminder that the USA was vulnerable too. Miss Somerset of course only emphasizes how much we ought to care by telling us we do not have to take the play seriously. She asks us to distance ourselves from the suffering of others because of their difference. We should not have to suffer the encounter with their suffering; they are not wholly human; they are alien; they are long ago or far away or just not us. By glibly articulating her stance ('you can always eat grass or something'), Miss Somerset only reinforces how continuously relevant the suffering of others, even the suffering of the past, must be to our present. When the stage manager and the actor playing Mr Antrobus insist that she continues the scene, she capitulates but establishes the intellectual stakes *via negativa*: 'All right. I'll say the lines but I won't think about the play.' Then, to us: 'And I advise you not to think about the play either.' Of course we do even more because she says not to. Perhaps the sense of a philistine ally makes the play's representations easier to stomach too.

Yet Miss Somerset's tears seem to come from a deeply humane (if deeply repressed) place. She does weep for the suffering of others; she just wishes she did not have to. She presumes that we may be similarly affected and wants to shield us from the suffering as she might shield children from having their innocence spoiled by the sight of death or sickness. The metatheatrical layer of the play, then, is infused with affect, not intellectual distancing. Rather than pushing us further away to reflect in objective distance, as Brecht's theatre did through many similar metatheatrical effects, Wilder's metatheatre draws us closer, makes us part of the action. We share in the struggle not only through identification or empathy; we have to help.

The characters' cataclysms leak down from the boards and into the auditorium. As the fire threatens to go out at the end of the first act, plunging the characters into the extinctions of the ice age, the family and refugees burn furniture to keep the fire going. Sabina asks that we help too, coming down to the footlights and addressing us directly: 'Will you please start handing up your chairs? We'll need everything for this fire. Save the human race. – Ushers, will you pass the chairs up here?'. They do: '*In the back of the auditorium the sound of chairs being ripped up can be heard. USHERS rush down the aisles with chairs and hand them over.*' The effect is thrilling, not just bringing the play into the auditorium but also the auditorium onto the stage and into the play. We see the very apparatus of theatre as our common human structure, one that must be united materially and psychically to continue existence. We must be ready to lose our seats to save the family. We must be ready to lose ourselves to history.

Miss Somerset, though, cautions against too much suffering in the theatre. She is not only averse to representing suffering; she is averse to representations that may cause suffering. In Act II, she interrupts not because she is too prudish to play out a scandalous love scene but because she does not want it to hurt one particular friend in the audience. When her character seduces the newly elected President George Antrobus on the Atlantic City Boardwalk, Miss Somerset insists on narrating rather than acting out the scene:

> Just a moment. I have something I wish to say to the audience. – Ladies and gentlemen. I'm not going to play this particular scene tonight. It's just a short scene and we're going to skip it. But I'll tell you what takes place and then we can continue the play from there on. Now, in this scene –

Naturally, the stage manager and her fellow actors grow angry with her. She is undeterred: 'I'm sorry. I'm sorry. But I have to skip it. In this scene I talk to Mr. Antrobus, and at the end of it he decides to leave his wife, get a divorce at Reno and marry me. That's all.' The stage manager insists she play the scene, but she says, 'there are some lines in that scene that would hurt some people's feelings and I don't think the theatre is a place where people's feelings ought to be hurt.' Her philistinism at least has heart:

> Well, if you must know, I have a personal guest in the audience tonight. Her life hasn't been exactly a happy one. I wouldn't have my friend hear some of these lines for the whole world. I don't suppose it occurred to the author that some other women might have gone through the experience of losing their husbands like this. Wild horses wouldn't drag from me the details of my friend's life, but . . . well, they'd been married twenty years, and before he got rich, why, she'd done the washing and everything.

Miss Somerset's comic failure of discretion would presumably hurt her friend more than a fictional representation, but there is something subversively affecting about it too. If the bourgeois theatre is a place to remain safe from traumatic personal memories and reminders of other people's suffering, Miss Somerset's antagonistic, rebellious and often mischievous interjections hardly offer an easier alternative. Instead of partaking in the sexual intrigue so common to Broadway spectacles, or the love scenes that manipulate our emotions and draw us into melodramatic theatrical pleasure, Miss Somerset interrupts the apparatus, refuses to perform this aspect of theatre and makes us step back. These interjections are the play's single most potent way of making direct contact with the audience. Miss Somerset is a thoughtful (though often wrongheaded) and compassionate (though sometimes harmful) subject coming to terms with theatre's representations and her ethical role as a performer. She actively seeks to save and shelter even as she reveals her anti-intellectual, anti-cultural methods as deeply flawed (and all too ubiquitous in mainstream commercial theatre).

Yet she is frequently necessary to prevent the play's dangerous excesses. Miss Somerset reins in the perils of the real. She most effectively intervenes to prevent physical harm to the actors. In Act III, George Antrobus returns home from the devastating seven-year war to confront his enemy son Henry. As they argue and then begin stage combat, they get carried away. In particular, the actor playing Henry goes too far. Miss Somerset, along with the actress playing Maggie Antrobus, runs on stage. 'Stop! Stop! Don't play this scene. You know what happened last night. Stop the play.' She reminds the actor playing Henry that he almost strangled the actor playing George at the last performance. Instead of urging her to let the action continue, the actor playing Henry reveals the source of violence and emptiness that may have led to such an inappropriate level of realism:

> I'm sorry. I don't know what comes over me. I have nothing against him personally. I respect him very much . . . I . . . I admire him. But something comes over me. It's like I become fifteen years old again. I . . . I . . . listen: my own father used to whip me and lock me up every Saturday night. I never had enough to eat. He never let me have enough money to buy decent clothes. I was ashamed to go downtown.

This actor describes a void, a traumatic emptiness in him that replays like trauma in a scene that cuts so close to the bone.

'Listen,' he says, 'it's as though you have to kill somebody else so as not to end up killing yourself.' The actor playing his father admits a related emptiness:

> Wait a minute. I have something to say, too. It's not wholly his fault that he wants to strangle me in this scene. It's my fault, too. He wouldn't feel that way unless there were something in me that reminded him of all that. He talks about an emptiness. Well, there's an emptiness in me, too. Yes, – work, work, work, – that's all I do. I've ceased to *live*. No wonder he feels that anger coming over him.

The actress who plays Maggie confirms: yes, the actor who plays George is indeed empty and a workaholic. But Miss Somerset denies the story from the actor who plays Henry. She says she knows his father and he was perfectly nice. Even as she denies the actor's subjective reality and memories, she somehow teases out a healing encounter by allowing the two men to see their mutual projections. She diffuses physical violence by getting them to talk about their feelings – but not just their emotional states: their animating forces, their acting out of behaviours they do not choose or understand. She allows the audience to see, through the act of acting, how profoundly and invisibly shaped all behaviour is by the past.

The play's most powerful failure to represent, even to go on, comes not from Miss Somerset demurring to portray or cause pain but instead from an incidence of 'real' abjection among the performers. Borrowing from his 1932 one-act play *Pullman Car Hiawatha*, Wilder stages (or 'tries' to stage) a procession that will gesture toward the literary and philo-sophical heritage of western civilization as well as the cosmos.

This time it is not Miss Somerset who interrupts but the stage manager: 'Miss Somerset! We have to stop a moment.' He calls for 'Lights, please', and asks the actor playing Mr Antrobus to explain. It turns out that several performers needed for this spectacle got food poisoning and, as Miss Somerset says, are 'having their stomachs pumped out this very minute, in perfect agony' at Bellevue Hospital. The actor playing George explains how the show will proceed without them:

> Naturally we haven't enough understudies to fill all those roles; but we do have a number of splendid volunteers who have kindly consented to help us out. These friends have watched our rehearsals, and they assure me that they know the lines and the business very well. Let me introduce them to you – my dresser, Mr. Tremayne, – himself a distinguished Shakespearean actor for many years; our wardrobe mistress, Hester; Miss Somerset's maid, Ivy; and Fred Bailey, captain of the ushers in this theatre.

These surrogates rehearse the procession that we will see again at the end of the play, but their version is necessarily compromised. They allow the audience to stay during the rehearsal but also suggest that we can leave, smoke or talk among ourselves. Every bit of theatrical magic is removed, laid bare. All that remains is a simple metatheatrical gesture. And even these 'splendid volunteers' are not enough to give the full scope of the cosmos. During the rehearsal the stage manager realizes 'The planets!! We forgot all about the planets.' We are told about a beautiful effect rather than seeing it:

> Ladies and gentlemen, the planets are singers. Of course, we can't replace them, so you'll have to imagine them

singing in this scene. Saturn sings from the orchestra pit down here. The Moon is way up there. And Mars with a red lantern in his hand, stands in the aisle over there – Tz-tz-tz. It's too bad; it all makes a very fine effect. However! Ready – nine o'clock: Spinoza.

Inviting our imaginative collaboration on the scene as he does so potently in *Our Town* (1938), Wilder celebrates the limits of theatricality and laughs at his own ambition. We are invited to laugh too, but also to appreciate it in a more imaginative way, to relish and complete the illusion with our imaginations and memories.

As for meaning, we see the actors and non-actors debate the significance of the procession of philosophers. The stage manager, ever pragmatic, tries to set up the scene:

[t]he author wants to show the hours of the night passing by over their heads, and the planets crossing the sky. . . uh. . . over their heads. And he says – this is hard to explain – that each of the hours of the night is a philosopher, or a great thinker. Eleven o'clock, for instance, is Aristotle. And nine o'clock is Spinoza. Like that. I don't suppose it means anything. It's just a kind of poetic effect.

In an ironic reversal, Miss Somerset protests in defence of the scene's meaningfulness: 'Not mean anything! Why, it certainly does. Twelve o'clock goes by saying those wonderful things. I think it means that when people are asleep they have all those lovely thoughts, much better than when they're awake.' But Miss Somerset's maid Ivy (the maid's maid, or meta-maid) offers the closest reading to Wilder's:

Mr. Fitzpatrick, you let my father come to a rehearsal; and my father's a Baptist minister, and he said that the author meant that – just like the hours and stars go by over our heads at night, in the same way the ideas and thoughts of the great men are in the air around us all the time and they're working on us, even when we don't know it.

This is as close as anyone gets to what Wilder himself might have said about the play's stakes, but it comes to us not as propaganda. We enjoy instead a relaxed self-effacing parody of meaning-making but also a genuine conversation about reading as an inconclusive, participatory act framed within a cosmos working itself out in performance. Our interpretations are welcome too. We are asked to think about the play's philosophical stakes but to allow our minds to explore different readings.

This metatheatrical layer also grounds the play in a cyclical experience of time that has much more to do with rehearsal than the linear mode of narrative (and history) often on display during any one particular performance. Not only do three cataclysms happen in three acts, implying an infinite potential repetition; the whole play ends where it began. After the parade of philosophers (the hours) and planets frames the reunited family tableau within an ever-flowing river of ideas and images, the curtain falls. When it comes up again, the domestic box set at the beginning has been restored. Sabina dusts the furniture, says her first line and then stops. '*She comes down to the footlights.*' Dropping into a reality somewhere between Sabina and Miss Somerset, she tells us, 'This is where you came in. We have to go on for ages and ages yet.' The play will go on, beginning again, again and again.

What Sabina/Somerset says is quite literally true when said early in a long run. The original production of *The Skin of Our Teeth*, directed by Elia Kazan, opened at the Shubert Theatre in New Haven in October of 1942, then moved to the Plymouth Theatre on Broadway for a run from 18 November 1942 to 25 September 1943. Throughout the run, many audiences came and went; even actors came and went. Tallulah Bankhead, for example, originated the role of Sabina but left the production in March 1943, replaced by Miriam Hopkins, then Gladys George, then Lizabeth Scott (Bankhead's understudy). Even since it closed on 25 September of the same year, the play has been widely remounted well into the twenty-first century. The cycle of replacement and substitution so central to theatre practice moves people through, putting new individuals in old roles. Such is life, too, Wilder seems to say, adopting theatrical production as both form and content. We replay old roles. The ancient struggles replay us as if we are actors. Yet we unconsciously make those roles into our present. We miss our essential repetitiveness. We cling to contingent identities that feel anything but. We carry on even when we do not know why or how.

Sabina/Miss Somerset/Tallulah Bankhead/Miriam Hopkins/Gladys George/Lizabeth Scott tells the audience to go home at the end. The messenger changes but the message repeats every night: go back to your own family, your own reckoning with the past and your own attempts to survive. What the spectator will miss when she leaves the theatre to the Antrobuses and to the many performances remaining is not blind, unchanging repetition though. The more things stay the same, the more they change. History continues. Performances repeat, with differences. We riff. Our response to each cataclysm is not unprecedented, yet neither is it merely a copy from a stale playbook. Each moment is shaped both by the roles we (re)play and by the infinitely becoming contingency of the present.

For all the play's repetitions and grafting of ancient roles onto modern situations, Wilder is anything but fatalistic. 'The end of this play isn't written yet,' Sabina tells us. We will continue working it out, as we have before, riffing on the past, repeating and changing it. As impossible as it sometimes seems, we move forward best by waking up each day reborn. We go forward by starting over. Sabina reaffirms our eternal role models: 'Mr. and Mrs. Antrobus! Their heads are full of plans and they're as confident as the first day they began, – and they told me to tell you: good night.' She bids us farewell on their behalf, wishing us the restorative sleep ('good night') that will bring us what the Antrobuses have in spades: tenacity. Like them, we will wake up. We will begin again. We will take on the world in all its impossibility, all its repetitions, all its cataclysms and difficulties. We will return to the blank stage or rehearsal room or workshop or office or construction site or household each day and live as if for the first time.

Wilder's metatheatre shows a world full of holes, unanswered questions and unknowable futures. By exposing the constructedness of theatre, of this very play, *The Skin of Our Teeth* allows us to enter the imaginative and material work of creating it. When we leave we can hopefully see the world outside the theatre as just as open for creation, inhabitation, play.

2

Metatheatre and modernism

Thornton Wilder developed *The Skin of Our Teeth*'s metatheatrical structure in the context of one of western theatre's most formally experimental periods. The early twentieth-century avant-garde performances and manifestos of European futurism, dada, surrealism, expressionism and new forms of dance transformed the boundaries of performance and deeply explored the essence of theatre through metatheatre. One of Wilder's most revered heroes and mentors, Gertrude Stein, contributed brilliantly to this experimentalism. She wrote 'landscape plays' that altered how spectators related to the temporality of performance. Her simple repetitive language and fragmented characters in operatic works such as *Four Saints in Three Acts* (1928) and *Doctor Faustus Lights the Lights* (1938) suggest dreamlike collages of myths, forces and interactions between states of consciousness that anticipate late twentieth-century experimental theatre such as that of Richard Foreman. Stein brought ancient, historical and mythic figures into a field of play with one another. She intermingled stage directions and dialogue, frequently omitting conventions of assigning certain words to specific characters.

She wrote characters who narrated their own actions and repeated phrases like sampled melodies. Wilder was always more logical and approachable than Stein, but he venerated her experiments with form and often pushed himself to meet her bold example.

Perhaps no playwright of the early twentieth century more explicitly explored the possibilities of representing theatre within theatre than the prominent Italian playwright and novelist Luigi Pirandello. Pirandello's most overtly metatheatrical plays, like *Six Characters in Search of an Author* (1921), *Henry IV* (1922), *Each in His Own Way* (1924) and *Tonight We Improvise* (1930), explore how metatheatre can help spectators unpack the theatrical nature of life. We see worlds that constantly reveal themselves as theatrical constructions. Actors and characters argue over the nature of truth and identity, frequently casting into doubt that there are any such realities except as relative, theatrical masks. Like Wilder, Pirandello posits a notion of self identical to its theatrical representations and everyday costumes. Theatre about itself as a medium helps Pirandello explore how constructed identity is, how performative. Pirandello may have modelled for Wilder a potent, psychologically sophisticated technique for creating cascading frames of reality. Like Pirandello, Wilder uses metatheatrical elements to examine the baffling complexities of being a subject whose identity is inevitably shaped by the past. Also like Pirandello, Wilder seeks an almost existential instability in the audience: he wants us to question what we thought we knew, caught between realities.

Unlike Pirandello, though, Wilder's stakes are not finally about the individual psyche and its 'empty masks'. Those masks are there only as part of the theatre whose ambition is the whole world. While Pirandello's instability often probes the psychological underpinnings of identity and what Anthony Caputi compellingly referred to as 'the crisis of modern consciousness' (Caputi, 1988), Wilder's seeks through this crisis to unpack the interdependent forces that make (and unmake) civilizations. Wilder's individuals are just elements and avatars – of ideas, forces, archetypes – as they shape and are shaped by a world in crisis. Put in a different way, his stakes are political if not quite didactic; they concern the community, the *polis*.

In that sense, Wilder's *The Skin of Our Teeth* in particular more closely resembles the political metatheatrics of epic theatre as developed by German director and playwright Bertolt Brecht, arguably the most influential theatre artist of the twentieth century. Although Brecht's early plays, such as *Baal* (1917), *Drums in the Night* (1922) and *In the Jungle of Cities* (1924) were wild, chaotic, bacchanalian works that embodied a rebellious, irrational and individualistic spirit, his later works, like *Mother Courage and Her Children* (1939), *The Good Person of Szechwan* (1941) and *The Caucasian Chalk Circle* (1944), were informed by his reading of Karl Marx. These pieces attempted to lay bare the mechanisms of society.

Written right around the 1942 premiere of *The Skin of Our Teeth*, Brecht's later plays used what he called the *Verfremdungseffekt* – often translated as 'alienation effect' or 'distancing effect', although a more appropriate translation might be the 'estrangement effect' or 'defamiliarization effect'. Influenced not only by Marx but also by the literary theories of Russian formalist critic Viktor Shklovsky, Brecht shifted from the individualistic chaos of early works to the notion that theatre operates best by taking the familiar and making it seem strange. A decisive transformation in his approach to acting came through his encounter with the Peking Opera performance of famous Chinese actor Mei Lanfang while in Moscow. Brecht saw in this performance tradition a fundamentally different approach to acting than the dominant styles in European theatre at the time. Brecht wrote that the Chinese actor does not 'become' the character or try to make himself experience the play's circumstances (as the nineteenth-century director Konstantin Stanislavsky influentially exhorted actors to do) but instead steps back, represents only the salient social gestures of the character, and provides a dialectical counterpoint by offering spectators the space to criticize choices and imagine how things could be otherwise.

Brecht's plays are punctuated by interruptions, metatheatrical frameworks, characters who temporarily act as other characters or step out of character altogether, and cascading frames of reality. He insists that his 'epic theatre' is fundamentally different from the 'dramatic theatre' described by Aristotle and championed influentially by the seventeenth-century Académie française in its insistence on neoclassical unities of time, place and action. Brecht's scenes are episodic, linked by ideas and narration rather than by a stable representation of a single place or an unbroken sequence of causally related events. Songs – emerging not from a swelling of the heart but from the need to interrupt and defamiliarize the action – step out from the established level of reality, cutting against the narrative flow. Banners announce scenes and give away the plot before it happens, removing the element of suspense and focusing us on the socioeconomic forces that shape behaviour and identity. Treadmills, wartime newsreel films and animations transform theatrical space into dissonant juxtapositions of different planes of reality.

Like Wilder, Brecht constantly reminds us that we are spectators at a theatre and that the illusion, such as it is, is constructed, not given. Like Wilder, Brecht suggests that the world outside the theatre is equally mutable, subject to human intervention. Both playwrights sought to empower spectators to think, criticize and understand the material underpinnings of life in an active way. They presented their theatrical worlds as propped up and full of holes, not subject to unchanging fate as in neoclassical tragedy, or the environmental determinism that underlies naturalism's hermetically sealed domestic scenes. Both playwrights also treated theatre like a public forum for sober, cheerful engagement with ideas rather than the hypnotic awe invoked by Wagner's operatic visions.

Wilder and Brecht were familiar with each other's work, and even planned to collaborate on an adaptation of *The Good Person of Szechwan*, although it never happened. As Douglas Wixson notes, Wilder was deeply interested in German drama. When his father was stationed in Hong Kong, the Wilders sent their son to a German school and he remained a reader of German literature throughout his life. In the German theatre, Wilder's works were very popular. Brecht also came into direct contact as an expatriate in the United States: he saw *Our Town* in New York. And, as Wixson notes, the two playwrights' staging techniques have much in common, including 'the projection of slides; the use of placards; the exposure of the stage's machinery (for example, the technical details of scene changing) to the audience's view' (Wixson, 1972: 122). This exposed apparatus promoted both the audience's collaborative role in creating the play and each spectator's ability to step back to see things from a more objective perspective (115). Both playwrights leave plays 'unfinished': Sabina tells us the 'end hasn't been written yet'; an actor, dropping character and walking down to the footlights at the end of

Brecht's *Good Person of Szechwan*, tells the audience that we have to finish the play ourselves out in the world. Both playwrights invite us to see the world like a theatrical production for which we are actors, directors and playwrights.

In this sense, Brecht and Wilder were engaged in a fundamentally related approach to theatre, and both powerfully explored metatheatre's potential to expose social mechanisms. They similarly embraced historical narratives of progress, and from a relatively optimistic perspective. Brecht's anti-fascist politics resembled Wilder's, although the two men would later be cast as the banner carriers for allegedly opposite ideologies: Soviet Socialism (Brecht was made the Artistic Director of the Berliner Ensemble in postwar East Berlin), and American representative democracy and capitalism (Wilder's plays made a tremendous amount of money on Broadway and are celebrated parts of high-school curricula, in part because of their patina of Norman Rockwell Americana). Brecht's concerns for the welfare of the downtrodden, hope in progress and sense of responsibility to history resembled Wilder's own far more than other metatheatrical playwrights of the early twentieth century – especially Stein and Pirandello, who both enjoyed patronage under fascist regimes.

Yet Wilder's attitudes toward modernity and human potential were fundamentally different from Brecht's. If Brecht interrupted our empathetic identification with characters to make us adopt an objective distance, Wilder interrupted to allow us to empathize ever more deeply – if not with a fictional character, then with her allegorical referent in repeated daily lives of billions, and in the soul of civilization itself. Wilder zooms out to humanity at large and indeed shows us the constructedness of all worlds, but not to give us a clear, logical tool whereby we can awaken into political consciousness and action. One never leaves a Wilder play feeling exhorted to protest or overthrow or *change* society. Rather, Wilder invites us to reflect philosophically such that we care ever more deeply and in more complex ways. For Brecht, the important thing about exposing the structure of things is to change things at a structural level. For Wilder, the important thing is to show how deeply interdependent, woefully misguided, joyously loving, touchingly hopeful and endlessly repetitive the world of human relations is. Like Brecht, Wilder wants theatre to allow us to see the world, and each other, as if for the first time, but to love it rather than dissect it.

Wilder shares Stein's sense of cyclical time and 'beginning again', Pirandello's notion that the self is a theatrical construction and Brecht's exposure of the mechanisms that underlie all social relations. *The Skin of Our Teeth* also brings something utterly singular: a clear-headed but baffling, often exuberant, meditation on the nature of life and death, on history, on our collective place in the universe. Wilder invites us to see the matrix but to feel a bittersweet empathy for the rise and fall of civilizations.

All four playwrights have had a powerful impact on theatre since the end of the Second World War. Not only are their plays reverently canonized in published collections and theatrical repertories all over the world; they have planted seeds that have grown into many of the most significant practices in European and American theatre of the past several decades. Since the 1970s, Stein's legacy has directly influenced the experimental plays and manifestos of the auteur Richard Foreman, who credits her for transforming how theatre shapes time and the unconscious. It is tempting to see Stein's traces also in the operas of Robert Wilson since *Deafman Glance* (1970), as well as the emptiness of language in the so-called 'theatre of the absurd' in the 1950s and 1960s. Pirandello's kaleidoscopic, indeterminate legacy is pervasive but most distinctively resurfaced postwar in the metatheatrical plays of Jean Genet and Peter Handke. Brecht's legacy has been arguably the most robust, varied and celebrated, from experimental political theatre to Broadway musicals. Along the way, Brecht's currents of influence have commingled and cross-pollinated with artists influenced by Stein, Pirandello and the historical avant-garde.

Wilder's piece of modernism's metatheatrical legacy is certainly part of this network of influence, but in *The Skin of Our Teeth* he creates something unique as well: the American fantasia on stage: an amalgam of European and American influences that brings mythic power to bear on everyday reality, that eclectically mixes genres and performance styles – colliding vaudeville with domestic realism, existential metatheatre with historical antiquarianism, folksy amateur theatricals befitting an elementary-school cafetorium with audacious Broadway spectacle (*Time* magazine called it a '*Hellzapoppin* with brains'), avant-garde experimentalism with cosy sentimental comedy. Wilder's influence lies in his peculiar juxtapositions. Digesting Europe's modernist strains, he transubstantiates them in such a way that a new, exuberantly modernist but entirely approachable world is born, a utopian (though endlessly difficult) promise of renewal in an imaginative collaboration with the audience.

In one sense, the theatre of Thornton Wilder, in all its eclecticism and layers of reality, resembles nothing more than a new kind of Elizabethan theatre. In *Great Reckonings in Little Rooms*, Bert States notes how Wilder's most scenically minimal plays, especially *Our Town*, resemble Shakespeare in their reliance on the spectators' imaginations to create the scenery (States, 1985: 97). In Shakespeare, places and things arise when needed, allowing an almost cinematic fluidity on the *tabula rasa* of the Globe stage. In Wilder, this world painted in words and gestures gives us a sense of our lives' fundamental transience:

> If furniture, streets, and houses are 'as fugitive, alas, as the years', then let us emphasize the fugitive status of these things in life; let us come right out and say that they don't matter; let us *see* that they don't matter; or, on still another level, let us see that we can see them without having them.
>
> (States, 1985: 97)

In many of Wilder's early plays, such as *Pullman Car Hiawatha* and *The Happy Journey to Trenton and Camden*, this Elizabethan scenic minimalism coupled with a rich texture of layered metatheatrical worlds creates literal journeys that allow us to use theatre as a virtual form of travel. These plays, like those of Shakespeare, can traverse the world so completely precisely by conducting our imaginations without the inertia of heavy scenic pieces; their journeys thereby rehearse the world's mutability. They also include the layered thoughts of characters like the soliloquies of Shakespeare. In Wilder's one-act plays, as well as in *Our Town*, minimalism facilitates his ambitious metatheatrical metaphysics.

Something else emerges in *The Skin of Our Teeth*, though – perhaps it better resembles Shakespeare's later stage of work at Blackfriars, wealthier and with greater technology for elaborate theatrics. Most obviously, *The Skin of Our Teeth* is anything but scenically minimal. The power of the work in performance depends largely on the force of its spectacle: glaciers, the Atlantic City Boardwalk and a home whose walls keep flying away to expose the mechanisms of modern theatre as a microcosm for the world. Instead of simply doing without the theatrical illusion, as George Gibbs and Emily Webb do in *Our Town* when they sit on ladders on an empty stage to represent their bedroom windows, the Antrobus family interacts in a house whose reality is all too grounded in the materiality of theatrical illusion. Instead of never having furniture and walls to begin with, *The Skin of Our Teeth* shows the constructedness of theatrical furniture and walls, how easily everything can come apart, washed away by time. By the time we really do have to use our imaginations, when all the theatrical effects fail and non-actors have to perform the procession of the philosophers, our souls take flight in our release from illusionistic scenery.

By conflating the mutability of the world with the mutability of its scenic constructions, by allowing us to see the artifice of theatre as a sort of objective correlative to the temporary structures of our lives, Wilder makes a modern world out of the old. He does for popular Broadway theatre what James Joyce did for the modernist European novel: he remixes and recycles at a fundamental structural level, putting into play the mythic, philosophical, scientific and spiritual forces inherent to the medium and its history.

That is no accident. Wilder greatly admired Joyce – particularly *Finnegans Wake* (1939), a notoriously difficult novel that Wilder famously 'deciphered' more compellingly than most. In fact, *The Skin of Our Teeth* so resembled elements of *Finnegans Wake* that Joseph Campbell and Henry Morton Robinson (1942) publicly accused Wilder of plagiarism in the *Saturday Review of Literature*. In a letter to the editor of the *Review* that he decided not to send, Wilder acknowledges that he was intrigued by Joyce's 'method of representing mankind's long history through superimposing different epochs of time simultaneously'. Although he abandoned an early sketch of a possible theatrical adaptation of *Finnegans Wake*, Wilder retained Joyce's 'idea of presenting ancient man as an ever present double to modern man', a fundamental basis for *The Skin of Our Teeth* (quoted in Tappan Wilder, 2003: 139).

The most significant difference between Joyce's novel and Wilder's play is that Wilder's material and medium – popular theatre – is made of more approachable stuff. While Wilder's short plays sometimes resemble the minimalism and staged streams of thought in the short plays of Joyce's onetime apprentice Samuel Beckett (who in fact transcribed *Finnegans Wake* while his mentor was going blind), *The Skin of Our Teeth* is more maximalism than minimalism and more farce than fringe. Wilder's very world is made of curtains and flats and stage managers. The kooky backstage antics provide the substance whereby Wilder tackles the coexistence of the ancient and modern, the 'superimposition' of epochs. For superimposition is inherent to theatre, its recycling of props and costumes, its repertoire of classics, its actors who famously played other parts, its repetitive structure of rehearsals and performances. Joyce's material, like Beckett's, was essentially the texture of thought itself, in part as explored through ancient and modern literature, but fragmented and strange. If the text of *Finnegans Wake* – or Beckett's *Not I* (1972) or *Ohio Impromptu* (1980) – is notoriously difficult, that is because the mind is impenetrable and contradictory. Beckett's late, short works in the 1970s and 1980s (like Wilder's one-act plays) find the fundamental texture of theatre in its limitations and capacity to distil lonely images in a void that highlights the materiality of thought.

The Skin of Our Teeth instead plunders the layers of thought that emanate from greasepaint, old costumes and stock conventions. Beckett's *Waiting for Godot* (1948) similarly explored the nature of boredom through two tramps who owe their patter to vaudeville comedians and the playful (though fundamentally empty) pratfalls and wordplay we use to fill the void, to entertain ourselves, to 'pass the time'. But *The Skin of Our Teeth*'s theatre uses even its repetitive structure to create an approachable (if ridiculously defamiliarized) family comedy that finds its metaphysics in a filling-up rather than emptying-out of theatrical artifice.

The result, infused with an almost quaint enthusiasm for human progress (naturally absent in Beckett), is a metatheatrical fantasia, an exuberant mixture of forms and styles that allows us to imagine world-making. *The Skin of Our Teeth*'s most metatheatrical tricks create a fascinating concentration of theatrical explorations from the past and pass them forward to the future. In response to his accusation of plagiarism, Wilder wrote that 'Literature has always more resembled a torch race than a furious dispute among heirs' (Wilder, 2007: xii). He passed along the torch of metatheatrical modernism to Tennessee Williams, Arthur Miller and beyond (see Konkle, 2006; Abbotson 2013).

The past three decades of American theatre have carried Wilder's torch in all kinds of explicit and invisible ways. Even beyond the direct use of *Our Town* in the Wooster Group's *Route 1&9* (1981) and Will Eno's play *Middletown* (2010), some of the most interesting and metatheatrical fantasias of the American theatre owe much to Wilder's vision. Among the dramatists who bear his legacy, probably no one has more directly credited Wilder than the author of *Baltimore Waltz* (1990) and *How I Learned to Drive* (1997), Paula Vogel. In her foreword to the 2003 edition of *The Skin of Our Teeth*, Vogel writes:

> For an American dramatist, all roads lead back to Thornton Wilder. Time and again, I return to his scripts and grapple with the problems he tackled – so, it seems, effortlessly – in the unwieldy theatrical apparatus. How do we, when we enter the theater, arrest time and make this art, made of actors and audience, the weight of scenery, flesh and face paint, melt into something fragile? How can we make the material mess of it all – rehearsals, tech, and opening night – disappear into spirit?
>
> (Vogel, 2003: viii)

Wilder gave American theatre its metatheatrical tools and basis in transcendence. The 'material mess of it all' transformed under his synthetic imagination into the spiritual source of freedom and tenderness we see in some of the most imaginative plays since the 1940s. Vogel first returned to Wilder's work after years of allowing his legacy to remain invisible to her – as it is to most of us, she writes, obscured by our memories of *Our Town*'s staid place in high-school and community theatre. Vogel goes so far as to acknowledge in plays like *The Skin of Our Teeth*, 'the roots or parallels of so many theatrical forebears and influences on [her] own work: Friedrich Dürrenmatt, Bertolt Brecht, Samuel Beckett, Arthur Miller, Edward Albee, Lanford Wilson, and John Guare' (ix). These figures resemble or even riff on Wilder, often so fully embracing his metatheatrical gestures that

Wilder's work invisibly saturates some of the most memorable moments in theatre:

> There, in *Our Town*, is the bold audience address I attributed to Tennessee Williams. There, in *The Skin of Our Teeth*, is the collapsing fragile box set exposing the family to the world that I remember in *Death of a Salesman*. There, also in *Skin*, is the nuclear family leaping across centuries and eras that I remember vividly in Caryl Churchill's *Cloud Nine*.
>
> (Vogel, 2003: x)

Likewise, Wilder's magical metatheatre and juxtapositions between the ancient and modern provide a template for some of the most interesting moments in Vogel: Li'l Bit's re-enacting of childhood traumas as she retells them as an adult, the use of a Greek chorus, the direct addresses to the audience. Wilder's influence was previously ignored by serious playwrights in favour of Brecht, Stein and Pirandello – in part, Vogel claims, because Wilder's influence is so ubiquitous, but also because we forget just how revolutionary his theatre was. Its radical form and audacity appeared just as entertaining, wholesome and sentimental as bourgeois audiences could ask for.

To Vogel's list we might add Tony Kushner's 'Gay Fantasia on National Themes', *Angels in America* (1993) – arguably the most influential American play since Tennessee Williams's *The Glass Menagerie* (1944) and Arthur Miller's *Death of a Salesman* (1949). Although Kushner most directly cites Brecht as an influence – and Brecht's formal ideas thoroughly imbue all Kushner's theatre (and metatheatre) – *Angels in America*, as James Fisher (1999) has noted, more than passingly resembles the scope and metatheatricality of *The Skin of Our Teeth*. *Angels in America* takes place in an imminent apocalypse, juxtaposes national politics around the AIDS epidemic with the personal lives of particular characters and includes a fantastical *coup de théâtre*: an angel with a tremendous wingspan who descends through the ceiling to render prophecy to a character in bed suffering hallucinations from AIDS complications. Kushner moves cinematically between scenes, and stages surreal, impossible dream sequences along with a serious philosophical reckoning with faith and suffering in Judaism, Mormonism, American democracy and the collapse of Soviet Communism. In *Angels in America*, Fisher writes, Kushner fundamentally shares *The Skin of Our Teeth*'s sense that suffering can make us more resilient and capable (Fisher, 1999). This strength from suffering – not only from social injustice but also from an honest engagement with the 'apocalypses' of 1942 and 1993 – is steeped in the power of our moral imaginations, our capacity to recognize the suffering of others, to find in their suffering a mirror to our own: a common bond and communal power born of reckoning with history's endless repetitions. Kushner's ambitious metatheatrical fantasia builds on the suffering of the apocalypse to renew the world, embracing the determination and positivity of *The Skin of Our Teeth* as a source for theatre as a place to bear witness, rethink things and rebuild.

We see Wilder's trace too in the brilliant repetitions and revisions (or 'rep and rev') of one of the boldest American playwrights since Kushner, Suzan-Lori Parks. Parks's *The America Play* (1994) takes place in an 'exact replica' of the Great Hole of History and follows 'the Lesser Known', an African-American man who leaves his job as a gravedigger to move out west and dress as Abraham Lincoln, allowing white tourists to quote John Wilkes Booth ('death to tyrants!' or 'the South will be avenged!') and 'shoot' him again and again in distinctly theatrical ways that distort even as they re-enact history. The play involves many metatheatrical elements, including direct audience address, a re-enactment of *Our American Cousin* (1858) (the play Lincoln was watching at the Ford Theatre when shot) and video addresses from a television screen. Parks primarily builds on the 'rep and rev' structure she sees as inherent to many African and African-American performance traditions, especially jazz improvisation, and eschews linear narratives in dramatic structure as complicit in the linear and oppressive way history is constructed. She also draws extensively on the complicated history of American theatre traditions – especially blackface minstrelsy – to deconstruct and explore identity. In all her plays, especially *The America Play*, Parks uses metatheatre in a way Wilder would deeply appreciate.

Whether Wilder directly influenced Parks (or Vogel, Kushner, Eno or Churchill), his fantasias on the repetitive nature of history established a particular kind of metatheatre that collides the personal and political, the everyday and cosmic, the ethical questions of how to live and love your family as they encounter the philosophical underpinnings of identity, community, history. Theatre's abilities – and, just as importantly, its limitations and repetitions – give these works their form and content at once, showing the new world emerging as a playground for ideas and speculative energy. The postwar metatheatrical fantasia as synthesized first and most powerfully in *The Skin of Our Teeth* asks its philosophical questions in and through the very materiality of theatre's props, costumes, fictions and audiences. Wilder makes of his metatheatre a microcosm for civilization as well as a bold metahistory that asks us to step back and see history as a constantly changing construction or constellation of forces.

Part II

Metahistory

3

Metahistory and myth

The Skin of Our Teeth telescopes a huge swath of western history and myth into a domestic family tragicomedy. As in *Our Town*, Wilder stages a kind of theatrical ode to daily family life in the face of mortality. If *Our Town* invokes equanimity and a renewed attention to the small stuff, *The Skin of Our Teeth* reaches outward, swallowing the world. In the latter play Wilder calls for audacious feats of staging and a wildly anachronistic amalgam of periods and mythologies smashed together so forcefully that the play tears at its seams.

Wilder calls for directors and designers to stage the ice age with its ominously approaching glaciers, right on the heels of the advent of the wheel and alphabet (Act I); a flood of literally biblical proportions that engulfs a convention for the Order of Mammals at the Atlantic City Boardwalk (Act II); and the aftermath of a devastating war that synthesizes elements ranging from the Roman Empire and Crusades to the French Revolution, Napoleonic Wars, First World War and (most pressingly for his first audiences) Second World War (Act III). Wilder's characters are thinly or not at all disguised versions of Adam and Eve, Lilith, the Sabine women,

Cain, Moses, Homer, the Muses, Socrates, Robespierre and Hitler. As mentioned, the play even ends with a parade of philosophers' ideas including quotes from Aristotle, Plato and Spinoza, as well as representative music from the spheres. Wilder pushes the apparatus of theatre to its limit as he tries to reproduce the history of the world and its ambition toward the cosmos.

The Skin of Our Teeth exceeds what theatre normally stages but does not aggressively break with tradition – as did much of the European avant-garde that influenced Wilder, especially the theatre and painting of futurism, which he encountered in Rome; his correspondence with his mentor and idol Stein; and his absorption in theatrical experimentation common to contemporaries like Pirandello, Brecht and others. Instead, Wilder stages a playful, often irreverent collage of myths drawn from the canon of western literature. The family embodies the Everyman characters Wilder often relies on to explore 'universal' human experiences. Throughout, he infuses into this family's adventures and tribulations a vast intertextual synthesis made of western culture's most canonical sources (Lifton, 1995).

From the beginning, Wilder grounds the ostensibly modern characters in ancient biblical archetypes. After narrating the break of day as if it were a major news event, a newsreel announcer helpfully alerts the audience that a ring was found in the aisles with the inscription: 'To Eva from Adam. Genesis II:18'. In a singing telegram sent from the 'office', where he invents civilization, George Antrobus wishes a happy 5,000th wedding anniversary to his dear 'Eva' (although elsewhere everyone refers to her as Maggie). George might easily be compared to most of the patriarchs of the Hebrew Bible, sometimes a transparent sign of Adam but with traces of both

Abraham and Noah as well – especially in Act II, as he saves his family and two of every creature from the Flood. The maid Sabina introduces Mr Antrobus as 'a very fine man, an excellent husband and father, a pillar of the church'; she insists that he 'has all the best interests of the community at heart'.

Biblical and ancient Greek figures intermingle playfully with modern life. George sends a telegram to his wife through a circuitous path that recalls the beginning of Aeschylus's *Agamemnon*, the first play of the *Oresteia* trilogy (458 BCE). 'This telegram was flashed from Murray Hill to University Heights! And then by puffs of smoke from University Heights to Staten Island. And then by lantern from Staten Island to Plainfield, New Jersey.' Rather than mimic the flame signals that declare the fall of Troy, Wilder transplants a primitive form of long-distance communication onto modern American towns (with a little Native American history tossed in). He also smashes the ancient together with the modern and transposes the tragic onto the banal.

The final act of the play takes place in the aftermath of every war, drawing its power from the cumulative force of history. The unspecified worldwide conflict urgently refers to the Second World War but also echoes the French Revolution and Napoleonic Wars, the Crusades, the Sack of Rome and the *Iliad* or *Aeneid*. Sabina may return '*dressed as a Napoleonic camp follower*' in '*begrimed reds and blues*' but behind the destroyed 1940s American home '*some red Roman fire is burning*'. Henry could be a peasant general or a Bolshevik, a Nazi or Napoleon: '*He is wearing torn overalls, but has one gaudy admiral's epaulette hanging by a thread from his right shoulder, and there are vestiges of gold and scarlet braid running down his left trouser leg.*' At the end of the play, we are left with tatters of western civilizations recent and ancient.

The seeds of western civilizations encoded in literature, philosophy and art leave traces that become relics. Luckily the books survive. George Antrobus values stories and ideas above all, particularly the lineage of the western canon, from Antiquity to the Enlightenment. Early in Act I, George's telegram advises his family in the face of the coldest July on record ('the dogs are sticking to the sidewalks', the maid Sabina says) to 'burn everything except Shakespeare' in order to keep the home fire going. His reverence for the Great Master of literary and theatrical wisdom reproduces his canonicity. He chooses and lionizes Shakespeare over others, but through Shakespeare also suggests his interest in a range of Catholic, Protestant and Jewish culture; ancient Greek and Roman thought; as well as homespun folk wisdom passed down in daily rituals between parents and children.

The play brings major intellectual and poetic figures of Antiquity literally into the modern Antrobus house in Excelsior, New Jersey. As the ice age begins in Act I, refugees approach the Antrobus home, seeking shelter from the glaciers. Against Maggie's caution, George insists the family welcome these great doctors, judges, teachers, professors, philosophers, poets, musicians – those needed to rebuild western civilization. Mr Antrobus introduces his wife to Judge Moses (who wears a skull cap), Homer (a blind beggar and singer-songwriter with a guitar), the Muses (three of nine sisters who teach music: Miss E. Muse; Miss T. Muse, Miss M. Muse), Hippocrates (with a serpent-clad staff) and Socrates (a professor). Homer recites the beginning of the *Iliad* in Greek after striking a chord on his guitar. Moses tries to comfort everyone with words from the Torah; he 'parts his hair and recites dramatically' in Hebrew. When the Muses sing against the advancing cold and dying fire, they do so with American folk songs that carry a distinctly mythic weight.

These ancient figures take comfort in human resilience writ large but concentrated in one family. The Antrobuses, their maid Sabina tells us, recently helped us survive the Great Depression 'by The Skin of Our Teeth' and have apparently revived civilization for thousands of years. The anachronistic community of mythic refugees gathers into the home of this family, where it projects itself into the future (our present) by stressing the education of their young. As the first act ends, the daughter Gladys Antrobus recites a Longfellow poem and Genesis; Henry recites multiplication tables. Together they convince their father that they, and we, are worth saving. The act ends with the beginning, so to speak, as Gladys recites: 'In the beginning God created the heavens and the earth; and the earth was waste and void; and the darkness was upon the face of the deep.' Meanwhile, the representatives of ancient Greek and Jewish civilization tear up their chairs for wood to keep the fire going – and Sabina exhorts the audience to do the same.

As Act II begins, the world has rebuilt, and even overbuilt, now teetering on the edge of excess, like Pinocchio's Pleasure Island or Las Vegas – or Gomorrah. Humanity relishes its recent success at a boardwalk that clearly stages Atlantic City in its timeless pleasures: gambling, dancing girls, theatrical spectacle. But the soothsayer Esmeralda, the only figure besides Sabina allowed to speak asides to the audience, reminds us that all this spectacle is illusory and toxic. The images of beauty queens and bingo parlours, chair-pushers and announcers, fundamentally distract us from an intentional, devoted life, she seems to suggest. Theatrical spectacle, in an almost Platonic sense, obscures the truth. We must incorporate our lives into

the lineage of history in order to pass the torch of civilization forward: also so that we may draw from its deep roots.
The boardwalk's distractions and excesses – commodified sex,
money, power, *theatre* – threaten civilization's progress with
stagnation and dissolution. The Antrobus clan grows morally
bankrupt without the trials of suffering that plagued (and
blessed) earlier, more difficult epochs. Looked at from one
angle, these decadent times are the late Roman Empire with
its gladiator fights, orgies and imperial hubris; looked at from
another, they are the Roaring Twenties with their flappers
and mobsters. They are also humanity (*anthropos*) fallen from
grace: every empire's most decadent phase at the peak of its
power, on the eve of collapse into chaos or feudal barbarism.

Esmeralda appears to be just another attraction at the
fair: the woman who can read your future for a price. But
her prophecies cut deeper and draw from ancient authority,
both biblical and pagan. She offers a secret history that often
contradicts the history of progress and triumph that President
George Antrobus crows and that the Boardwalk celebrates.
Cassandra-like, Esmeralda sees the future but cannot stop it
or convince anyone to listen. Gypsy-like, Esmeralda also can
see how and when individuals will die, tapped into the mysterious foreknowledge of the Fates. She may even suggest
something like the Apollonian Oracle, sought out by Sabina
for advice on her destiny with George. Esmeralda shares the
playwright's foresight and contact with the audience. She
speaks to us directly, bursting through the barrier between
worlds, and leads us like an American Protestant preacher. She
is abused by those who will not believe her. The celebratory
drunkards and party people pooh-pooh her revelations, laugh
at her and call her a 'Jeremiah'. Jeremiah was the Bible's second great prophet, one who saw impending destruction as a

result of the people's sins. He warned everyone that excess has consequences. Like a biblical prophetess as great as Jeremiah, Esmeralda foretells the Flood as a retribution for worldly wickedness: 'You know as well as I what's coming. Rain. Rain. Rain in floods. The deluge. But first you'll see shameful things – shameful things.' She appeals to us, the audience, as potential judges, a community responsible for upholding values, for bearing witness. But like both Judaic and Christian communities, we are not only there to relish God's wrath. 'Some of you will be saying: "Let him drown. He's not worth saving. Give the whole thing up." I can see it in your faces. But you're wrong. Keep your doubts and despairs to yourselves.' We the community are cast as righteous in our perspective, but flawed. We must also draw upon Jewish and Christian notions of redemptive suffering; we must have faith in the potential for George Antrobus to reconcile with God and rebuild again, this time with humility.

Embedded in the notion of redemptive suffering is a model of history: one that ends in final judgment. This model of history is also the structure of *The Skin of Our Teeth*. The apocalyptic events that befall the family (and the rest of the world) replay the Flood three times in three acts, but the most literal comes in Act II. As Esmeralda prophesies, the world will go on only by safeguarding its seeds: 'Even of the animals, a few will be saved: two of a kind, male and female, two of a kind.' Nor is she the only one who sees dark skies ahead. Maggie Antrobus notices a threat to the family in her husband's eagerness to spend too much on temporal pleasures, like rides for the kids or the bingo parlour. She tells George to be careful with money; they must be good stewards of their wealth to prepare for darker times. 'Mark my words, a rainy day is coming. There's a rainy day ahead of us. I feel it in my bones.'

Even the modern storm-signal technology registers the progress of the apocalypse. George explains to Henry that 'One of those black disks means bad weather; two means storm; three means hurricane; and four means the end of the world.' Maggie, uneasy, goes to buy raincoats; Henry keeps his eye on the boat at the end of the peer. As the flood comes, George orders his family, along with two of each animal, onto the boat, escaping the drowning revellers just in the nick of time.

This apocalyptic, or eschatological, version of history relies on a fall from grace: a temptation in the garden, a transgression against the good. John Milton's *Paradise Lost* gives vivid image to this narrative: Lucifer and his followers, through pride, caused a heavenly war and a rift in the once-harmonious universe. Ever since, humankind has repeated this traumatic fall again and again, from Adam and Eve tasting the apple to western societies growing decadent. Of all the threats to civilization's moral core, few are more clearly personified in Wilder's play than the erotic lure of extramarital sexual pleasure and the egocentric excesses of pride. Sabina, the maid from the previous act, has acquired a new personality by the top of Act II. Now called Lily Fairweather, her name suggests a 'fairweather friend', one whose 'friendship' will not survive a cataclysmic change of 'weather'. More importantly, she channels the figure of Lilith from the Talmud Bavli, or Babylonian Talmud – Adam's first wife who was made of the same clay and who has come to represent both the dangers of powerful women and a model for feminist movements. Lilith, according to medieval Midrashic literature, was the first woman and first wife, coequal with Adam, born from the same stuff. Eve only later replaced Lilith, as a more servile model of womanhood.

Wilder's Lily Sabina Fairweather of Act II channels the mythic figure of Lilith in especially theatrical ways and insists on her place in history. She wins a beauty pageant judged by none other than the newly elected President Antrobus. She connives to seduce him with the help of the soothsayer and prophetess Esmeralda. All the men and boys follow Lily with their eyes when she walks by. She performs a femininity at the intersection of desire and power. Young Henry Antrobus tries to see her undress in her beach cabana. Gladys Antrobus tries to emulate Lily by wearing lipstick and buying scandalous red stockings, finally waking her father up to Lily's dangerously theatrical influence.

Not merely an object of the male gaze, Lilith also represents a fiercely intelligent – and, to certain men, inscrutable – subject who can use her charms to change the world with her words. She paints for George an elitist picture of their mutual exceptionalism. As he ponders how Maggie might feel when he leaves her, Lily Sabina responds:

> [O]ther people haven't got feelings. Not in the same way that we have, – we who are presidents like you and prize-winners like me . . . . Listen, darling, there's a kind of secret society at the top of the world, – like you and me, – that know this. The world was made for us. What's life anyway? Except for two things, pleasure and power, what is life? Boredom! Foolishness. You know it is. Except for those two things, life's nau-se-at-ing.

This theatrical temptation stands in for a more general temptation to abandon our responsibility to history in favour of pleasure-seeking in temporal things – although Lily sees it differently: a deep responsibility to meritocracy, to George's own genius and power, his (and her) enjoyment of their fruits. Lily particularly arouses his impulse for decadence through juxtaposition, casting the world of the home as no life at all – far beneath the smart, sexy lives they are destined to lead. In a sense, Sabina only carries through on her rivalry with Maggie Antrobus in Act I, when she notes defiantly that 'it is girls like I who inspire the multiplication table'. Maggie, Sabina says, 'is not a beautiful woman' and not the rightful partner to the great man George Antrobus. Lily demands her place in history.

History has obviously been quite bad to women. For the mythic Lilith, Lily's seduction represents Adam's return: to their equal primal sexual union, to their original dance – back before marriage, children and leadership burdened him with responsibility and left her dispossessed, on the margins of the sacred union (and history). Yet Wilder's Lily Sabina has other ancient roots, too, in another mythic paradigm at the dawn of the Roman Empire that authorizes the subjugation of women. Sabina is most obviously named for her deeply colonized origins, as in the 'Rape of the Sabine Women' wherein Romans in the eighth century BCE mythically kidnapped women of the Sabine hills for 'wives' and thus peopled the original city. As Maggie reminds Sabina in Act I, when George 'raped' her from her 'Sabine Hills, he did it to insult' his wife. Even Sabina's novelty eventually lost its lustre, resulting in a new status as servant and enemy to the nuclear family. This aspect of the Sabina character makes her hard to dismiss. Her attempts to leverage sexual desirability for material gain come from a context in which she was traumatized by deep injustices, horrible suffering and ancient yet persistent power imbalances. In Maggie's depiction of events, Eve remains the Wife in every sense of the word; Sabina is no Lilith but instead a Cassandra, a captured woman brought home as concubine, for ever cut off from her roots and now just the maid, just a slave.

In this sense, her character embodies a marginalized history of women, used but yet shut out from the history as written by and about men. Theatrical stereotypes, as generations of feminist thinkers have noted, leave women little agency or nuance: there are fewer female roles; they largely conform to types such as 'supportive wife', 'young ingenue', 'mother', 'whore' or 'vengeful monster'; and these roles have historically left many real women cut off from roots or authentic expression.

Sabina is certainly rootless, drifting between characters and fortunes from act to act. When the actress Miss Somerset interrupts the action she contrasts Sabina's theatrical Lilith-like qualities with her own prim refusal to say certain lines, perform certain scandalous acts with George or generally get on board with Wilder's work – which she does not care for and frequently insults ('I don't understand a word of this play'). What Miss Somerset has in common with her character Sabina is a sense of being on the outside looking in. Sabina is the always-dependent cast-off, marginalized from dominant History. She remains the eternal 'other woman' yoked to the powerful leaders of humanity, the Antrobuses. Sabina's potential power, such as it is, lies only in her exotic and erotic otherness and in her capacity to perform, although always before the gaze of the 'great man'. She has little access to the feminist legacy of Lilith except as a sort of returning soldier in Act III, when she no longer orients herself by the male sign of Antrobus. Even then she returns to her household chores and praises George's victory over dark forces, his share of History. Miss Somerset is her only way to break out of her role and resist the patriarchal narrative – including especially its theatrical fetishization and subjugation of women.

Maggie Antrobus, instead of Sabina, gives women's history its only vocal political representative in the play. At the top of Act II, she shares the stage with her husband and upstages his popularity when the announcer adds to George's inventions (the alphabet, mathematics, the wheel, beer) her own (the hem, the gusset, silk, frying in oil). Maggie speaks to the gathering, invoking a time before marriage as a dark age filled with rapacious barbarism. She calls the ring a great achievement for women's rights:

> Each wedding anniversary reminds me of the times when there were no weddings. We had to crusade for marriage. Perhaps there are some women within the sound of my voice who remember that crusade and those struggles; we fought for it, didn't we? We chained ourselves to lampposts and we made disturbances in the Senate, – anyway, at last we women got the ring.

She appears like a powerful suffragette even though for her the stakes are so firmly rooted in the home. She opposes President Antrobus's 'watchword' of the year – 'enjoy yourself!' – with her own: 'Save the Family!'. Though her share of civilization may seem condescendingly domestic, she also makes an eloquent case for the women left out of History. That capital-'H' History, the master narrative that makes the chaotic coherent and authorizes the rule of the powerful, includes the stories we tell on stage – especially this one. As George tells his wife he is leaving her for Lily, Maggie throws a bottle into the sea:

> And in the bottle's a letter. And in the letter is written all the things that a woman knows. It's never been told

to any man and it's never been told to any woman, and if it finds its destination, a new time will come. We're not what books and plays say we are. We're not what advertisements say we are. We're not in the movies and we're not on the radio. We're not what you're all told and what you think we are: We're ourselves. And if any man can find one of us he'll learn why the whole universe was set in motion. And if any man harm any one of us, his soul – the only soul he's got – had better be at the bottom of that ocean, – and that's the only way to put it.

Wilder gives voice to the very impossibility of an authentic woman represented in history or in a man's play. In this moment, Maggie – or the actress playing Maggie – drops a source of wisdom that underlies yet eludes the canon (even as men obsessively try to write and perform women). Eve is shut out: from biblical authority, from becoming a true literary protagonist, from historical power, even from *The Skin of Our Teeth*. She echoes a longing we see in Sabina and Gladys too. Although he acknowledges that women in cultural production are ever idealized and transformed into images for male consumption, Wilder does not hesitate to put Maggie Antrobus on another kind of pedestal: the Virgin Mary, Gaia, Earth Herself.

The flip side of the women bulldozed by history are the men behind the bulldozer. Wilder creates his most destructive avatar of male chauvinism in Henry Antrobus, the couple's only (surviving) son. If anyone embodies the historical harm men cause, it is he. Marked with a scar his mother can never completely hide beneath his hat or scrub off ('sometimes

I think that it's going away – and then there it is: just as red as ever'), Henry is haunted by his previous name:

> Mama, today at school two teachers forgot and called me by my old name. They forgot, Mama. You'd better write another letter to the principal, so that he'll tell them I've changed my name. Right out in class they called me: Cain.

Maggie recoils at the reminder, desperate to gloss over and move on, to reintegrate this lost soul back into society. When the refugee Judge Moses later asks after her other son, though, Maggie cannot help but mourn his loss in a cry from her soul that comes out more like a lamentation than speech: 'Abel, Abel, my son, my son, Abel, my son, Abel, Abel, my son'.

Not long after, Henry/Cain is at it again. He kills the neighbour boy with a rock, allegedly to keep him from stealing the giant stone wheel his father recently invented and brought home. He escapes his father's wrath only through his mother's intervention to remind her husband 'how young he is': 'only four thousand years old'. But Henry appears irredeemable. In Act II, he kills again, this time targeting a black chair-pusher at the Atlantic City Boardwalk, right before the devastating Flood. By the time he enters the war-torn ruins of his family home in Act III, after some kind of Great War has ended, he has become the embodiment of western violence, carrying with him resonances of marauding killers, upstart white supremacists, fascist revolutionaries, Robespierre, Napoleon, Hitler, Mars: war itself. From the rubble of the house, Sabina tells Henry's mother and sister (who had no idea) that Henry is no longer welcome there according to Mr Antrobus. Henry reportedly was quite good at being bad, rising 'from corporal to captain, to major, to general. – I don't know how to say it, but the enemy is *Henry*; Henry *is* the enemy.' Accordingly, he is also cast as a human avatar of Lucifer, not just in the sense of evil but in the sense of absolute rebellion, total refusal to fear and obey his father or to incorporate himself into 'His' ideas and values. Henry blames his father's books for the ideology he rejected and wants to annihilate the ancient regime.

Multiple versions of history intersect: the legacy of the ancients, the story of technological progress, the history of intellectual thought, the omitted history of women, the history of war and destruction. Beyond this tapestry of historical narratives, *The Skin of Our Teeth* also attempts to stage natural history. (Or rather, it attempts to stage this necessarily failed attempt to stage natural history.) 'Nature' appears on epochal scales as well as in small creatures. The Antrobuses have a pet bird in a tiny cage, but also a pet mammoth and baby dinosaur, played by actors in ridiculous costumes more appropriate for sports mascots than dramatic characters. When Maggie first enters the domestic scene of Act I, she asks Sabina if she has 'milked the mammoth'. George praises the animals for not talking too much, after which they both repeat a regular refrain: 'I'm cold.' The Antrobuses allow these animals in from the cold and enjoy their company as if they were a cross between cows and dogs. They depend on each other and take care of each other. These now-extinct representatives of non-human creatures then become the sacrifice required to keep humanity alive, the bullocks at the altar. Maggie insists that the refugees (Homer, Moses, the Muses, *et al.*) can come in, but only if the dinosaur and mammoth go. They are expelled from the safe enclave of the four walls, left to die in the oncoming ice age. The humans retreat and build fires that protect them from the elements, but they do so through a radical fissure from the rest of creation.

Human history runs parallel to but distinct from natural history. As President Antrobus takes his leadership at the top of Act II, he addresses humanity as embedded within the natural order. He acknowledges the extinction of the mammoth and dinosaur but glosses over the cause: human exceptionalism mixed with cold pragmatism. It is the 6,000th annual convention of the 'Ancient and Honorable Order of Mammals, Subdivision Humans'. Representatives of sea- and sky-dwelling creatures come too to hear him speak. But George must defend his humanity, as distinct from non-human, particularly non-mammalian, life: 'I do not deny that a few months before my birth I hesitated between . . . uh . . . between pinfeathers and gill-breathing, – and so did many of us here, – but for the last million years I have been viviparous, hairy and diaphragmatic.' He simultaneously speaks to pre-natal science and Darwinian natural selection, thereby showing both our common heritage as evolving organisms and our fundamental resemblance as living creatures. At the same time, he firmly reinforces his biological likeness to his kind as against (and racially superior to?) non-mammalian creatures. His insistence on genetic or morphological difference contains the seed of violence and radical separation.

Maggie identifies with a more undifferentiated version of history exemplified by the sea; like the sea, she remains shut out from the very culture she gave rise to but mourns it and seeks reconciliation. She looks forward to seeing the whales and constantly scans the horizon. (Henry, not surprisingly, has a more violent relationship to the animals: he shoots at ducks with his slingshot.) At the end of the act, after his tryst with Lily, the president must address the radio audience – all the world – but he stops when he sees the representatives of whales and birds who have come to witness. They remind

him of Maggie and his daughter Gladys, those who sought
a meaningful connection to nature on this family vacation.
The animals thereby remind him who he is and what he must
do: he gathers the family; spurns Lily Sabina Fairweather; and
ushers two of each elephant, kangaroo, wolf, jackal and turtle
onto the distant Ark. He takes his place not only as part of
creation but also as its chief steward, responsible for ensur-
ing the future of the environment. He trumps natural history
with human history, justifying a new dominion.

The history of human civilization, though, necessarily falls
apart once it flies too close to the sun. Not even Wilder's
mythic sources can convincingly capture the far reaches of
time and space. As the play reaches outward beyond the earth
it shows how simultaneously feeble and resourceful theatre
can be when it meets its limits. Borrowing the parade of philosophers from Wilder's short 1932 play *Pullman Car Hiawatha*,
Act III stages a procession of hours as if performed by beautiful girls dressed as Elihu Vedder's Pleiades and holding roman
numerals for each hour of the night. In *Pullman Car Hiawatha*
Wilder also tries out a prototype of Emily Webb's 'goodbye,
world' speech made famous in *Our Town*. A woman on the
train dies overnight and has to bid farewell to her life. *Our
Town* unspooled this thread into understanding an individual
life and death. *The Skin of Our Teeth* instead teases out the earlier play's abstract ideas, celestial bodies and time itself in the
procession of the hours, gesturing beyond the individual to all
that we cannot understand. While Wilder's figures pass along
a raised platform they recite Plato, Aristotle, Spinoza and the
Bible. There is also an orchestral performance of the solar system, with planets and the sun and moon. But we do not actu-
ally get to see this ambitious reach to the heavens and through
outer space. It is ultimately unstageable. As mentioned above,

the stage manager has to come out to tell us that the performers got food poisoning, and then rehearses their replacements
in front of us: the captain of the ushers, a dresser, a maid,
a stagehand. The result is a deliberately amateurish rehearsal
and restaging that highlights its insufficiency for the task. The
stage manager even has to do without the planets at all, telling
us to use our imaginations.

In that sense, the procession of the hours, days, years and
planets is a synecdoche of the whole play: a testament to the
vastness of the universe and history's necessary failure ever to
capture it in its totality. The canon of human knowledge and
creativity is vast far beyond any play's ability to represent it.
And humanity is vast, far beyond what any history can ever
represent. The mysteries of our religions and rituals are vast
beyond any story's capacity to make them cohere. The earth
is vast far beyond humanity and any religion's metaphysical
scope. The solar system is vast beyond earth, and the galaxy
vast beyond that. Theatre's insufficiency, *The Skin of Our Teeth*
suggests, is also its great strength: a finger pointed skyward, it
suggests by implication all that it does not and cannot stage.
Wilder stretches theatre to the breaking point to swallow and
stage all that is, was and will ever be. The absurdity of such an
attempt only shows how noble and touching it is to try – and
how necessary it is to do so with humility.

4

Metahistory and myopia

For all his audacious reach outward – through time, across cultures and epochs, into the west's deepest myths, around the vortex of gender, out beyond humanity and even the planet – Wilder concentrates the play's sprawling history into one white, patriarchal, heterosexual, Protestant (US-) American nuclear family. In order for the play to pull together vast difference into a coherent world and universalizing image it expels the very diversity it imagines. The entire world is reduced to Excelsior, New Jersey during the middle of the twentieth century. Although we meet many other people, the plot focuses on the most influential family on the planet and follows that family's personal relationships, heartbreaks and triumphs. As for the 'other' people we meet, even the refugees of Act I are hardly marginal: they include only the most influential thinkers and prophets of the West (Homer, Moses and so on). And as for history, here it is staged at its most western, patriarchal, hegemonic and white. Wilder posits the mid-century American nuclear family with its trials and triumphs as paradigmatic of all people's struggles everywhere. The play's overtly Protestant values stand in for values as such.

The play begins with a slide show and announcer: 'NEWS EVENTS OF THE WORLD'. From the beginning, it advertises radical inclusion but from a very particular perspective. Like wartime newsreels, it has gravitas and the promise of geopolitical significance. But it brings that scope into local (northeastern United States) scale. It begins with an image of daybreak – '*Slide of the sun appearing over the horizon*' – and the announcer's voice: 'Freeport, Long Island. The sun rose this morning at 6:32 a.m. This gratifying event was first reported by Mrs. Dorothy Stetson of Freeport, Long Island, who promptly telephoned the Mayor.' The cosmic stakes find quaint quarters, not far from the Antrobus home in Exelsior, New Jersey. Not that it is a slow news day. Glaciers are coming, and their impact affects tangible nearby victims: '*Slide representing a glacier*'. The announcer denies rumours that 'the ice had pushed the Cathedral of Montreal as far as St. Albans, Vermont', although the slide suggests otherwise. Wilder brings our attention not only to geographic proximity but also to the perspective of each theatrical production: '*Slide of the front doors of the theatre in which this play is playing; three cleaning* WOMEN *with mops and pails*'. We must recognize just how local our perspective is: we are an audience watching a play in this theatre about the whole world – as it comes to bear on this 'quintessential' American family (as a condensed representative of western culture at large). '*Slide of a modest suburban home*'. We see and hear about this family that at once accomplishes 'great leaps for mankind' and scales them down to an approachable suburban level:

> The home of Mr. George Antrobus, the inventor of the wheel. The discovery of the wheel, following so closely

on the discovery of the lever, has centered the attention
of the country on Mr. Antrobus of this attractive suburban residence district. This is his home, a commodious
seven-room house, conveniently situated near a public
school, a Methodist church, and a firehouse; it is right
handy to an A and P.

This homeyness presumably helps us identify with the protagonist and imagine our own families dealing with matters
of tremendous import to civilization. But of course that is a
perspective grounded in a culturally and politically hegemonic stratum of society: the white, mid-century, affluent
American nuclear family living in the northeast. George
'comes from very old stock' (ha ha) but 'has made his way
up from nothing', fulfilling a capitalist ethos built on pulling
oneself up by one's bootstraps.

George and Maggie Antrobus, named for 'human', anticipate the wholesome tenacity of television sitcom families like
Father Knows Best, but also the dark secrets and violence that
undergird mid-century American family dramas by Arthur
Miller and Tennessee Williams. Their secrets are far from
innocent, including not only infidelity but also rape, murder,
fratricide, genocide and the destruction of species. There is a
fascinating paradox at the heart of the Antrobus clan. On one
hand, the play situates them as the Platonic ideal of saviours,
inventors and leaders of humankind; on the other, the men in
particular (George/Adam and his son Henry/Cain) embody
all the violence of history. The play distils the brightness and
darkness of human culture into a 'typical' American nuclear
family that it handles both sentimentally and comically. This
very American family reflects what the play does as it stretches

beyond its capacity to contain all places and times: it reproduces in miniature the power, violence and cultural narcissism inherent in representing history in American theatre.

The set may represent red Roman fires, glaciers and the ocean, but in the first and last act it is confined to the world as it affects the four walls of the Antrobus house (the fourth removed, according to which naturalistic custom we spectators can voyeuristically observe). Though riddled with asides and outlandish spectacle, the play also pays homage to the domestic realism championed by Henrik Ibsen, Anton Chekhov and other late-nineteenth-century realistic European playwrights. In fact, the outside world most clearly relates to the domestic setting by rupturing it. At the beginning, walls and windows keep flying out via the fly system, exposing the means of making theatre even as they show a home whose integrity is in flux. With glaciers approaching, refugees and huge animals pouring in and fires going out, the home is the sanctuary whose instability only proves its importance. We are invited to join the family empathetically, to care that the domestic set remain whole, that the family remain whole. (Of course, we are also allowed to relish its disasters as a spectacle suffused with visual pleasure.)

The family who occupies this unsteady home is stretched to the breaking point by holding too much history. The five millennia of the Antrobus marriage witness the West's greatest feats and sorrows, which are themselves insufficient to the much greater world left out of western history. Nothing of Confucius, Buddha, Mayan art or West African dance appears, nor do the truly disenfranchised in the West, the beggars and victims of war. Of the great western monotheisms, Islam makes only a small, passing appearance. Wilder only focuses on the wealthy leaders of Christendom, but in *The Skin of*

Our Teeth he also makes us aware of that phenomenon. The Antrobuses relationship to that which is not at the centre of their universe is problematic, filled with rape and murder and all sorts of cruelty. Yet Wilder does not invite us to judge them harshly either; we are drawn into their home and see the world through their eyes. Their sins are ours too.

We spectators are cast as the Antrobus family, and not only because they supposedly represent all humankind. Wilder's original 1942 audiences at the Shubert Theatre in New Haven and the Plymouth Theatre on Broadway ('The Great White Way') were exemplary of the United States of America's most elite upper-middle-class theatre patrons. Yale faculty and students, Manhattanites with disposable incomes, suburban couples from New Jersey ('the bridge and tunnel crowd'), the literati who championed the play – or those well read enough to accuse Wilder of plagiarizing Joyce's *Finnegans Wake*: these were the kind of people who could identify with the Antrobus family without necessarily seeing this identification as culturally contingent. Nor are we spectators reprimanded to check our privilege. Rather, we are invited to take it for granted and understand it as the 'universal human condition'. Even if we do not individually partake of such wealth or power or European heritage, Wilder presumes a gaze that understands such power as natural and inevitable, even quintessentially human.

One does not have to dig too deeply to see the holes in Wilder's apparent glorification of the American middle class and western history. What happens to Sabina (for instance) is unfair, and is blatantly revealed as such. The fact that the actress Miss Somerset refuses to go on or perform scandalous scenes as written points to the uneasy relationship between the macrocosm and microcosm of Wilder's *theatrum mundi*.

We see this elsewhere in the impossibility of realistically staging glaciers, whales, floods, wars and planets. The events and
violence and excess of history will not fit within the whole
(domesticated) world of the play without making it burst at
the seams. Throughout, the play breaks down, questions its
own possibility and stages its failures. Its metatheatre manifests
its metahistory: the constructed and contingent perspectives
that produce any understanding of the past. Underlying both
Wilder's metatheatre and metahistory, though, is a deep structure to reality itself, a metaphysical reckoning with being.

Part III

Metaphysics

5

Metaphysics on parade

As George Antrobus gathers his tattered books at the end of
The Skin of Our Teeth, he tells his wife Maggie that along with
the opportunity to begin again, he thanks God for 'voices to
guide us; and the memory of our mistakes to warn us'. He
relishes the fact that 'We've learned. We're learning. And the
steps of our journey are marked for us here.' Crucially, the
journey is marked in a book that encodes its trajectory toward
the legacy of the ages. George stands by a table, leafs through
its pages, and recalls the darkest days of the seven-year war:

> Sometimes out there in the war, – standing all night on
> a hill – I'd try and remember some of the words in these
> books. Parts of them and phrases would come back to
> me. And after a while I used to give names to the hours
> of the night.

He finds the passage in his book: 'Nine o'clock I used to call
Spinoza. Where is it: "After experience had taught me –"',
but Fred Bailey, holding the IX roman numeral, finishes the
thought as the first of the procession:

> After experience had taught me that the common occurrences of daily life were vain and futile; and I saw that all the objects of my desire and fear were in themselves nothing good nor bad save insofar as the mind was affected by them; I at length determined to search out whether there was something truly good and communicable to man.

That something – an 'eternal totality' arrived at through reason – inspired some of the most provocative philosophical thought since the seventeenth century. Spinoza's *Ethics* (1677) has been singularly influential in philosophy's most insightful (and difficult) thinking, from Hegel to Nietzsche to Deleuze. Within the context of his life excommunicated from the Jewish community in Amsterdam, and of the European Enlightenment's reckoning with the groundbreaking work of Descartes, Spinoza sought truth through radical breaks with theological and philosophical orthodoxy. He was excommunicated by his religious tradition for heretically disputing God's anthropomorphism in the Tanakh, or Hebrew Bible (Old Testament). He sought God not in the ideas behind creation but in creation itself, which for him was identical with God. The mind of God does not create the world; it *is* the world. All that is is made of one undivided substance with infinite modes. Rather than remain committed to distorting ideologies or irrational responses that imbue the world with 'good' and 'evil' forces, Spinoza establishes a metaphysics and ethics rooted in the world.

Descartes helped; the older philosopher's emphasis on reason and rigorous logic gave Spinoza a method to strip scripture of its literal truth-claims. Descartes's *Cogito ergo sum* ('I think therefore I am') emboldened Spinoza to pursue an ambitious ontology removed from received articles of faith, freed to ask incisive questions about the nature of Being in itself. In a gesture bolder than any in seventeenth-century thought, Spinoza imagined a wholly impersonal God whose manifestation in the world happens not through supernatural intervention but instead through the totality of natural laws. Both invoking and collapsing Descartes's mind/body dualism – which posits that thought and matter are fundamentally separate – Spinoza articulates the nature of the human mind in ways that even eighteenth-century Enlightenment thinkers found challenging. Rather than the Cartesian mind (or spirit) that thinks or enacts its will upon an essentially inert body (or object), Spinoza wrote that thought and 'extension' were merely two modes of the same substance.

Spinoza's sense of substance imbues the (meta)theatrical world of *The Skin of Our Teeth*. From the domestic walls that continuously tilt, fly away and return, to the glaciers that encroach upon the home and the sea that threatens the Boardwalk, Wilder's set appears to have a mind of its own. Characters relate to the scenic world not as subjects who confidently behold or manipulate objects but as continuous with its thought. The cataclysms, renewals and metaphysical reflections of the play surge through the visible, physical world – of which characters are crucial but not dominant parts. Although the implied author looms and the stage manager interjects, they do not stand apart from 'Creation' as creating subjects. The stage manager is flummoxed by the failures and vicissitudes of performance; Wilder negates his own presence by framing a play that becomes itself through performance, radically contingent and with immanent thought.

The implications of Spinoza's thought were not only ontological but also ethical. If everything that exists is fundamentally made of the same stuff, and all of that is one and the same with God, then who are we to impose our will on others – even other life forms, or even objects? We cannot, as Cartesian thought compelled, treat the world as separate from ourselves or 'mere' matter, without thought. Since everything is fundamentally both thought and extension, there is no such thing as a pure thought removed from matter. Nor, for that matter, is there any such thing as a thing without thought. Not only do all creatures think; all things are part of thinking, are integral to mind. That Spinoza's posthumous *Ethics* uses his ontological and epistemological claims to set up how one ought to behave is significant. What for Nietzsche amounted to Spinoza's vital removal of morality as an absolute code (God is dead, so we are free) also grounded the ethical in a constant negotiation with others. This reorientation challenged the divine right of kings, the great chain of being and the notion of an external authority to please. Instead, Spinoza's *Ethics* grounds the good life in understanding and conforming to human nature. We should, as all things, be. For human beings, whom he saw as rational, that meant rational contemplation of the world and the absolute freedom to think. The best kind of society (for Spinoza, liberal democracy) would permit its citizens to self-actualize and would work itself out practically, in an ever-evolving negotiation with and through the world as it is. Like Maggie and George Antrobus – and the constantly shifting metatheatrical apparatus that keeps reinventing civilization as if it were a perpetual rehearsal – Spinoza's preferred state would be up for debate and revision. It would not aspire toward a Platonic-ideal utopia; it would work itself out again and again, forever. Rather than an end, or *telos*, this is a universe whose repetitions and catastrophes are all we have.

This constant revision and working out animates both the texture of Wilder's visual world and the rhythm of beginning again. As Sabina says in Act III, as Maggie and she begin to repair and reset the domestic scene from the war-torn rubble, 'That's all we do – always beginning again! Over and over again. Always beginning again'. Recalling the scenic instability of the first act, she pulls the rope that causes a portion of the wall to return to its position. Sabina questions the whole effort of beginning again in the face of the inherent meaninglessness and repetitiveness of existence. She sounds more like Schopenhauer than Spinoza:

> How do we know that it'll be any better than before? Why do we go on pretending? Someday the whole earth's going to have to turn cold anyway, and until that time all these other things'll be happening again: it will be more wars and more walls of ice and floods and earthquakes.

But Mrs Antrobus returns her to the task at hand: 'Sabina!! Stop arguing and go on with your work.' Though Sabina submits the effort to scrutiny, the act of work imbues the world with the only meaning it will have. The only *telos*, 'end', is in our encounter with each other and the stuff through which we partake in world-making.

Wilder's inclusion of Spinoza as the first philosopher might suggest an anti-Platonic commitment to becoming over Platonic Being, but then Hester walks by with the roman numeral X, quoting Plato on the microcosm he sees in the leadership of the *polis*:

> Then tell me, O Critias, how will a man choose the ruler that shall rule over him? Will he not choose a man who

has first established order in himself, knowing that any decision that has its spring from anger or pride or vanity can be multiplied a thousand fold in its effects upon the citizens?

Plato, the West's first philosopher to create a truly systematic philosophy, famously founded the Academy in ancient Athens where he expounded on the ideas and dialectical method of his martyred mentor Socrates, wrote dialogues and developed his theory of forms. In *The Republic* and *Critias* (as well as other dialogues) Plato sees the state as a macrocosm for the individual. The ideal state would produce the ideal citizen, and, reflexively, be led by the ideal ruler: the philosopher-king who, undeceived by mere appearances, seeks the Truth – the ideal Form – of which individual entities are merely imperfect copies. For Plato, the ruler's interior 'order in himself' can be achieved by climbing up the philosophical ladder toward ever loftier notions that precede (and produce) all things. This leader must not get entangled with representations – 'thrice removed from reality' – or emotional passions. The ideal leader controls her passions through reason, not gathered as new knowledge but instead recalled from the world of forms forgotten among the muck of matter, our world of shadows. Plato's ideal state, like his ideal citizen and ideal leader, would love justice as an intrinsic good: the proper balance and interaction among reason, spirit and desire. (It would, significantly, have no place for illusionistic theatre.) This Truth, originating in an immutable and usually invisible real, differs sharply from the practical ethics of negotiation and becoming; it seeks Being itself as the source of what one should become and do.

Plato's metaphysics jibes with Wilder's ancient archetypes replayed in endless particulars. George and Maggie Antrobus are not just an exemplary couple; they are the Platonic ideal of *anthropos*, humankind. Their struggles are not just comparable to our own; they are echoes of the same root forms. Their society, rooted in Excelsior, New Jersey (the Platonic ideal of an American town on the eastern seaboard, whose name is etymologically connected to excelling beyond the ordinary) proves its ideals through seemingly infinite reiterations. George becomes the model of patriarch, inventor, political leader; Maggie is Eve and Mary, motherhood itself; Sabina is sex and mischief; Henry is violence; Gladys is innocence always on the verge of getting lost in sexual compromise. In Plato, as in Wilder, there seems to be an ultimate reality and even an ideal state one might aspire to. Plato's influential mistrust of representation in general and theatre in particular even finds an echo in Wilder's theatrical representations which always fall apart, distinctly secondary to the abstract ideas they point toward.

Above all, the leadership of George Antrobus always depends on his ordered self. Henry is the ultimate rebel against the ideal state his father constantly attempts to establish, preserve and rebuild. As he rises to the top of the rebellion, Henry defies the order of the *polis*, and even as he returns in Act III, beaten and exhausted, he wants to kill everything George's leadership stands for. He compares living within this order to '[s]tanding like a sheep at the street corner until the red light turns to green', and deplores the 'stinking ideas' his father gets out of books. Henry sees nothing in George's power and hierarchy but oppression and inequality: 'what have they done for us? . . . Blocked our way at every step. Kept everything in their own hands'.

George responds to Henry's rebellion much as Plato critiqued democracy as a political system – and the

democratic citizen as a human being. The primacy of freedom that democracy espouses allows its citizens to pursue
their desires rather than the good. Far from liberating, the
democratic world enslaves people to their base drives, fos-
tering pleasure and gratification over wisdom. Moreover,
Plato's argument goes, democracy is destined to devolve
further into tyranny, for ultimately only the most violent or
most flattering to the public will lead, not the philosopher
king who would orient society toward wisdom and virtue.
Henry fails to articulate any positive formation of democracy, and it is clear from his father's words that the rebellion
he led was far from egalitarian and ultimately depended on
a chaotic power grab without an orientation toward taking
care of the populace:

> How can you make a world for people to live in, unless
> you've first put order in yourself? Mark my words: I shall
> continue fighting you until my last breath as long as you
> mix up your idea of liberty with your idea of hogging
> everything for yourself. I shall have no pity on you. I shall
> pursue you to the far corners of the earth. You and I want
> the same thing; but until you think of it as something
> that everyone has a right to, you are my deadly enemy
> and I will destroy you.

What is the 'same thing' that father and son both want? Clearly,
they are both invested in some notion, or energy, related to
improvement, but Henry's energy is led by libido rather than
the well-ordered mind George (and Plato) sees as led by reason. George ultimately wins the day, as always. Rather than
destroying his son, though, he reincorporates him back into
the fold, metonymically reining violent passions into the

world order. George reifies and plans to manifest his utopia. As Sabina says:

> Mr. Antrobus is still thinking up new things. – He told me to give you his love. He's got all sorts of ideas for peacetime, he says. No more laziness and idiocy, he says. And oh, yes! Where are his books? What? Well, pass them up. The first thing he wants to see are his books. He says if you've burnt those books, or if the rats have eaten them, he says it isn't worthwhile starting over again. Everybody's going to be beautiful, he says, and diligent, and very intelligent.

Based on learning and thinking through the ideas passed down from Antiquity, George plans to make of the population ideal citizens. Their freedom will not be the licence on gratuitous display on the Atlantic City Boardwalk of Act II; rather, these 'beautiful, . . . diligent, and very intelligent' citizens will be freed from unwholesome passions to become their best.

Yet Wilder's universe draws from Aristotle as well as Plato. His archetypes do not pre-exist their human avatars, nor is the abstract where their ultimate truth lies. In other words, the fundamental reality of things happens before us – not elsewhere, not in heaven, not at the end of the play, not in final judgment. Not even, necessarily, within the fiction of the play – the metatheatrical outer layer keeps reminding us that these actors are people too who, like their characters, are trying to deal with the world as it appears. Faced with repeated apocalypses, the Antrobuses must save humanity based on what they see before them: glaciers, floods, the carnage of war. It is not the underlying ideal of these catastrophes that unites them but the thinking mind that recognizes in their repetition a pattern. Particular manifestations do reveal a cosmic structure, but not one whose reality is an immaterial form floating above in heaven. Far from it: the experience of the play constantly brings us spectators back to our seats, back into direct contact with actors, set pieces, outlandish costumes, the very stuff of theatre.

The play's grace is not external to it, despite its gestures beyond what it can possibly represent. Instead, *The Skin of Our Teeth* stages grace as the divine spark in each human mind as it contends with the world's particularity. Through creation (the wheel, society), service (sheltering refugees) and stewardship (of animals, of children, of books and history), Wilder's characters sometimes tap into divinity, and inspire his spectators to do the same. After Plato's quote passes, Ivy, Miss Somerset's maid, quotes Aristotle, the eleventh hour:

> This good estate of the mind possessing its object in energy we call divine. This we mortals have occasionally and it is this energy which is pleasantest and best. But God has it always. It is wonderful in us; but in Him how much more wonderful.

We are not occasionally divine because we (occasionally) reflect goodness in our imperfect ways. Rather, we can see in our best acts the spark of divinity. We can see the world along with our creativity and thinking as emanating divinity, not as a pale imitation but as an extension continuous with God – a name given to Aristotle's notion of 'a prime mover' who set everything in motion. Aristotle's *Metaphysics* (at least as read by thirteenth-century scholastic theologians such as St Thomas Aquinas, who made a monotheistic version of Aristotle's body of work central to Catholic thought) sees properties not as abstractions but as immanent to the world as it reveals itself to us – and more importantly, in our acts, our speech, our discernment. The ability to get closer to the divine happens not by turning away from the world but by understanding it ever more deeply, by attending to and thinking about it, by acting in and through it. Though Aristotle, like his friend and mentor Plato, revered philosophical reflection, he also – like George Antrobus – recognized the good life possible in participating in the political sphere.

To forge ahead, George Antrobus consults influential if contradictory models of metaphysics without attempting a synthesis. He returns finally to the 'Beginning' – in Genesis: 'In the Beginning, God created the Heavens and the earth; and the Earth was waste and void; And the darkness was on the face of the deep. And the Lord said let there be light and there was light.' This is not the first time; Gladys recited the same words at the end of Act I, but without the last line ('And the Lord said let there be light and there was light'). The final 'philosophical' quote departs from the thought of Spinoza and the pagan thought of Plato and Aristotle. Like Augustine or Aquinas, Wilder frames philosophy within Christianity. Rather than reasoning toward ethics through ontology or a cohesive metaphysical system, the procession of the hours ends with midnight: the final hour but also the first hour, the start of a new day. Rather than building on or beyond the philosophers, the procession ends with a return to a beginning, to sacred history. Wilder both implies a kind of ultimate biblical truth and forecloses the apocalyptic or at least teleological direction implied by Judeo-Christian eschatology.

6

Metaphysics and the end of history

Spinoza, Plato, Aristotle and the Bible largely represent contrasting metaphysical systems. Plato and Aristotle long occupied philosophers and theologians as metaphysical opposites (though Aristotle owed much to his former teacher). Spinoza transcends them both, while utterly rejecting the myths of Judeo-Christian history and inspiring the decidedly secular character of modern philosophy. Genesis may predate all of these thinkers, but the Church as Wilder encountered it formed in part through a reconciliation with and synthesis of Plato and Aristotle.

What these systems had in common was a commitment to a linear, teleological and even apocalyptic (or eschatological) notion of history and metaphysics. Judaism narrates origins and prophetic returns. Plato sources the flow of truth in ideal forms and anticipates the completion of human progress in the ideal state. Aristotle suggests that the world does not end but that humans progressively actualize through science and philosophy, through negotiation, through knowledge. Even the secular humanism expanded through the Enlightenment in the wake of Descartes and Spinoza tended toward finality, progress and completion: the dialectical progress of history in Hegel and Marx, the technological utopias and triumph of capitalism in liberal democracy. Each metaphysical system uses itself up in its realization, so that even without a godhead we reach something like apocalypse and a new world, at least a sense that thinking gets us somewhere.

Wilder gives this linearity and eschatology vivid shape. His apocalypses are literal and looming. From the beginning of Act I, the mysterious advancing of the glaciers and primitive inventions spell trouble that the rest of the act must keep at bay. From the beginning of Act II, prophecies warn of the flood. From the beginning of Act III, a new world, a kind of Zion, beckons in the charred aftermath of war. Myths and histories are brought together and synthesized; the philosophers come to us through a linear progression; the play gestures toward its own ending and makes us aware that beginnings and endings are crucial.

Yet through the very act of repeating its apocalyptic structure (in triplicate), Wilder shows that each end is just another beginning. Like theatre, like history, we start over. All the linear, end-directed energy reaches some form of completion or annihilation, but what feels like apocalypse is never really final. As Sabina tells us to go home, she says that the actors and stage managers and crew will keep repeating the play for ages. Such is the nature of theatre. Each production is made of repeated performances. Each performance is made of repeated rehearsals, which are themselves structured on repeated moments. Each instance of a play produced repeats each previous instance, and each play written contends with the canon, its repetitions, the endless echoes of civilizations that rise and fall: humans who are born and die, spectators who understand everything they see based on everything they have ever seen.

Wilder's metatheatre establishes a metaphysics rooted in his metahistory. The nature of being as such lies not in singularity, nor in ideal forms, nor in substance. The nature of being lies in repetition. It is through happening *again* that being arises: one *is* a Maggie or a Sabina insofar as her words and acts echo. That is not because there was some *ur*-Maggie (Eve) or *ur*-Sabina (Lilith) to whom all future repetitions owe their existence. 'Eve' and 'Lilith' only arise in retrospect, when future people's thoughts and actions rhyme and invite us to look backwards. Nor is the ultimate reality the perfection of the form, the ultimate realization of the perfect woman or man or the perfect society.

Rather, in the deep circles and spirals of our repetitions we can see how theatrical the world is, how much its coherence as a world amounts to its echoes and rhythms. By happening again, with differences, and by making that repetition manifest, each concrete particular transcends its particularity. As universals arise, however, distilled from each concrete particular, they feed back into the world; they structure it; they give us the capacity to recognize patterns and even our yearning to make the world better. So the universal and particular produce each other in a never-ending cycle, a kind of Möbius strip of abstraction and concreteness, archetype and individual life, historical structure and messy events, metaphysics and metatheatrics, text and performance, without separation. Wilder's model for history and the deep structure of being lies in theatre's always-changing *pas de deux* between representation and matter.

The Skin of Our Teeth does not politically urge a radical departure from western paradigms of linear progress. In a sense, such an exhortation would only reinforce their linearity and teleology by suggesting that a new, better idea ought to replace the outdated notions. Similarly, for all its obsessions with the past the play does not seem to yearn for a golden age lost to the entropy of time. Instead, Wilder swallows and replays the West's apocalyptic historiography and metaphysical structures. He shows us the reenactment at the heart of historical and personal being.

Through its exuberant metatheatre and audacious metahistory, *The Skin of Our Teeth* turns the apocalypse inside out. It suggests a metaphysics that, like theatre, depends neither on absolute origin nor on absolute terminus. Instead, Wilder proposes a world that resets each hour at midnight. The progress of thought resets in each re-enactment of prior thoughts. The actuality of the world is rooted neither in ideal form nor in inert matter but in repetition, rhythm, renewal, reanimation, recycling, recovering, reworking, remaking, reawakening, re-enacting, resetting the scene. Our place within this world lies in our performance and revision of it – not just because we are microcosms of the world's theatrical unfolding but because, as Spinoza might say, our repetitions are the very substance and meaning of the world itself.

References

Abbotson, Susan C.W. (2013). "To the American Clock by the Skin of Our Teeth," in Thornton Wilder: New Perspectives, ed. Jackson R. Bryer and Lincoln Konkle (Evanston: Northwestern University Press).

Aeschylus (1984). The Oresteia, trans. Robert Fagles (London and New York: Penguin Books).

Aristotle (1998). The Metaphysics, trans. Hugh Lawson-Tancred (London and New York: Penguin Books).

——— (2006). The Poetics, trans. Joe Sachs (Newburyport, MA: Focus Publishing).

Beckett, Samuel (1954). Waiting for Godot (New York: Grove Press).

——— (1973). Not I (London: Faber and Faber).

——— (1989). Three Plays: Ohio Impromptu, Catastrophe, and What Where (New York: Grove Press).

Brecht, Bertolt (1966). Mother Courage and Her Children, trans. Eric Bentley (New York: Grove Press).

——— (1999). The Caucasian Chalk Circle, trans. Eric Bentley (Minneapolis, MN: University of Minnesota Press).

——— (2008). The Good Person of Szechwan, trans. Ralph Manheim and John Willett (London and New York: Penguin Books).

——— (2015). Brecht Collected Plays, Vol. I: Baal, Drums in the Night, In the Jungle of Cities, and Life of Edward II of England, ed. and trans. John Willett (London and New York: Bloomsbury Methuen Drama).

Campbell, Joseph and Henry Morton Robinson (1942). 'The Skin of Whose Teeth?', Saturday Review of Literature 25: 3–4.

Caputi, Anthony (1988). Pirandello and the Crisis of Modern Consciousness (Urbana and Chicago, IL: University of Illinois Press).

Churchill, Caryl (1984). *Cloud Nine* (London: Taylor and Francis).

Deleuze, Gilles (1988). *Spinoza: Practical Philosophy*, trans. Robert Hurley (San Francisco, CA: City Lights Books).

Descartes, René (2013). *René Descartes: Meditations on First Philosophy. With Selections from the Objections and Replies*, trans. John Cottingham (Cambridge: Cambridge University Press).

Eno, Will (2010). *Middletown* (New York: Theatre Communications Group).

Fisher, James (1999). '"Troubling the Waters": Visions of the Apocalypse in Wilder's *The Skin of Our Teeth* and Kushner's *Angels in America*', in *Thornton Wilder: New Essays*, eds M. J. Blank, D. H. Brunauer and D. G. Izzo (West Cornwall, CT: Locust Hill Press), 391–407.

Joyce, James (1966). *Finnegans Wake* (New York: Viking Press).

Konkle, Lincoln (2006). *Thornton Wilder and the Puritan Narrative Tradition* (Columbia, MO and London: University of Missouri Press).

Kushner, Tony (2014). *Angels in America: A Gay Fantasia on National Themes. Revised and Complete Edition* (New York: Theatre Communications Group).

Lifton, Paul (1995). *'Vast Encyclopedia': The Theatre of Thornton Wilder* (Westport, CT and London: Greenwood).

Miller, Arthur (2015). *Death of a Salesman* (London and New York: Bloomsbury Publishing).

Milton, John (1900). *Milton: Paradise Lost* (Edinburgh and London: W. Blackwood and Sons).

Parks, Suzan-Lori (1995). *The America Play* (New York: Dramatists Play Service).

Pirandello, Luigi (1957). *Naked Masks: Five Plays by Luigi Pirandello*, ed. and trans. Eric Bentley (New York: Plume Books).

Plato (2000). *The Republic*, ed. G. R. F. Ferrari, trans. Tom Griffith (Cambridge: Cambridge University Press).

Savran, David (1986). *Breaking the Rules: The Wooster Group* (New York: Theatre Communications Group).

Shakespeare, William (2016). *Hamlet: Revised Edition*, ed. Ann Thompson and Neil Taylor (London: Bloomsbury Arden Shakespeare).

Shklovsky, Viktor (1965). 'Art as Technique', in *Russian Formalist Criticism: Four Essays*, trans. Lee T. Lemon and Marion J. Reis (Lincoln, NE: University of Nebraska Press).

Simmel, Georg and Helmut Loiskandl (1991). *Schopenhauer and Nietzsche* (Chicago and Urbana, IL: University of Illinois Press).

Spinoza, Baruch (1985). *The Collected Writings of Spinoza*, trans. Edwin Curley (Princeton, PA: Princeton University Press).

States, Bert O. (1985). *Great Reckonings in Little Rooms: On the Phenomenology of Theater* (Berkeley, CA and Los Angeles: University of California Press).

Stein, Gertrude (1934). *Four Saints in Three Acts* (London and New York: Random House).

——— (2005). *Doctor Faustus Lights the Lights* (Alexandria, VA: Alexander Street Press).

Vogel, Paula (1992). *Baltimore Waltz* (New York: Dramatists Play Service).

——— (1998). *How I Learned to Drive* (New York: Dramatists Play Service).

——— (2003). Foreword to Thornton Wilder, *The Skin of Our Teeth* (New York: Perennial Classics), vii–xiii.

White, Hayden (1973). *Metahistory: The Historical Imagination in Nineteenth-Century Europe* (Baltimore, MD: Johns Hopkins University Press).

Wilder, Tappan (2003). Afterword to Thornton Wilder, *The Skin of Our Teeth* (New York: Perennial Classics), 123–53.

Wilder, Thornton (1997). *The Collected Short Plays of Thornton Wilder*, 2 vols (New York: Theatre Communications Group).

——— (2003a). *Our Town* (New York: Perennial Classics).

——— (2003b). *The Skin of Our Teeth* (New York: Perennial Classics).

——— (2007). *Three Plays* (New York: Perennial Classics).

Williams, Tennessee (1999). *The Glass Menagerie* (New York: New Directions Books).

Wixson, Douglas C., Jr. (1972). 'The Dramatic Techniques of Thornton Wilder and Bertolt Brecht: A Study in Comparison', *Modern Drama* 15: 112–24.

Index